CYCLING
Touring Guides

WITHDRAWN

Nº 5 CENTRAL ENGLAND

HAROLD BRIERCLIFFE
WITH MARK JARMAN

BATSFORD

ACKNOWLEDGMENTS

Thanks to Sam Howard at Sustrans for providing details of the latest
Sustrans routes, and to Ruth Briercliffe for her assistance.

First Published 1949
(under the title *Cycling Touring Guides: The Midlands*)

Revised edition published 2012 by

Batsford
10 Southcombe Street
London W14 0RA

An imprint of Anova Books Company Ltd

Volume © Batsford, 2012
Additions by Mark Jarman and Sustrans

The moral rights of the author have been asserted.

ISBN-13: 9781849940405

A CIP catalogue record for this book is available from
the British Library.

20 19 18 17 16 15 14 13 12
10 9 8 7 6 5 4 3 2 1

Reproduction by Mission Productions Ltd, Hong Kong
Printed and bound by Toppan Leefung Printing Ltd, China

CONTENTS

LIST OF LINE ILLUSTRATIONS

LIST OF PLATES

4

INTRODUCTION

The *Britain by Bike* TV series was based on a collection of old and largely forgotten cycling guides written by Harold Briercliffe over 60 years ago in the late 1940s. Such was the interest in the TV series and associated book that the guides quickly went from almost unknown on the second-hand market to much sought after and almost impossible to obtain. Perhaps the main reason for the renewed interest in the guides is that they take you back to a time many now see as cycling's golden era. They are so much more than slightly dated books with directions to help you find your way from A to B. Indeed anyone who sought out the original *The Midlands* guide in the belief that it would provide accurate and reliable information about the best cycle routes around Central England will be rather disappointed. Clearly, as a 21st-century cycling guide, Harold Briercliffe's writings are no longer as helpful as they once were as so many aspects that impact upon cycling conditions have changed dramatically since the 1940s. For this reason, in this revised reissue the end of each chapter includes details of current recommended Sustrans routes that can be used to help explore the places that Briercliffe visited on his cycle journeys. The real joy of Harold's original books is their insight into Britain in an earlier age and a reminder of a gentler pace of life and the attractions of cycle touring around Britain.

The starting point for understanding and appreciating the guides is to look at the context in which they were written. In the post-war years, Harold Briercliffe was a writer for *Cycling* magazine, then the UK's main cycling publication. The guides were assembled from the feature articles written in the magazine, with each issue covering an area of the UK that later formed the basis of a chapter within the regional guides. The first guide was published in 1947 and covered the Northern England region. Over the next few years a further five were produced ending with the *Southern England* guide, which was published in 1950.

The post-war Britain that Briercliffe encountered on his cycling journeys was a place in the midst of austerity, where rationing strictly controlled the availability of essentials, including food, clothes and fuel. It is worth remembering that at the end of the 1940s only 1 in 7 households had access to a car. If you were one of the few that did have a car your family's vehicle was likely to have little in common with today's air-conditioned people carriers and 4 x 4s. The most popular cars of the day were rather uncomfortable and modestly sized by modern standards with the Morris Minor and the Austin A30 being two of the most popular 1950s models. For most people, the main methods of mechanised transportation were rail, bus and, of course, the bicycle. With the average workers' holiday being only one or two weeks a year, the bicycle was seen as a key form of transport, offering cheap and easy access to the UK's places of interest (alongside bus and rail travel). During this period, the UK's cycling industry output was moving towards its peak. There were numerous manufacturers producing bicycles not only for the domestic market but for export all over the world. Notable companies from that era include Phillips, Dawes, BSA, Holdsworth, Royal Enfield, Elswick, Sunbeam, Evans, Claud Butler, Bates and Hetchins. But it was Raleigh that became established as the leading bicycle manufacturer of the day with the company's bicycle production reaching a peak of over a million in 1951. This increase in demand and supply was accompanied by advances in design so that bicycles became much more suited to longer distance touring. The use of lightweight 531 tubing to build the classic diamond-shaped frame (including randonneur handlebars), and the introduction of the simplex derailleur gear system and cantilever brakes, meant that the bicycles available in the early 1950s looked remarkably like modern touring bikes (although today's bicycles benefit from more sophisticated alloys of steel and aluminium as well as a much greater range of gears and better pedals).

For those who might have been slightly less enthusiastic about spending their leisure time on a bike, there was relatively little to encourage them to stay indoors. This was a world without games consoles, personal stereos, home computers or wide-screen TVs. By the beginning of the 1950s only 8% of households in the UK had a TV. For the few television owners, there was only one station (ITV did not join the BBC until 1955) and the broadcasting hours were very limited. So for the vast majority, the radio 'wireless' provided the main source of family entertainment within the home. Cinema was the only other boom area for entertainment.

Against this background of ongoing rationing and limited forms of entertainment, it is perhaps easier to understand the reasons why Harold Briercliffe (approaching 40) embarked on the monumental task of covering the whole of the UK by bike. Following production of the *Northern England* guide in 1947, Briercliffe's articles in *Cycling* magazine were gradually used to form a series of regional guides covering the Scottish Highlands, Wales, South West England, and The Midlands before finishing with Southern England.

The Midlands guide, which in this revised edition we have renamed *Central England*, covered an enormous area of the UK that went well beyond the confines of more standard definitions of that region. He defined it as starting at the northern edge of the Cotswolds and continuing as far north as the River Mersey. The western boundary of the region was rather imprecise but considered to be a rough line joining Chester, Hereford and Newport. And the eastern boundary of the region seemed to use the Great North Road linking Doncaster down towards Newark and Grantham, eventually joining Huntingdon and Ware before going all the way to the Thames at London Bridge. As Briercliffe accepted 'The Midlands then, for the purposes of this guide, constitutes a far-flung region.'

Many parts of this central area of Britain have experienced significant changes over the last 60 years, particularly in terms of housing and traffic growth. Briercliffe suggests the use of what are now very busy 'A' roads to cycle out of main urban areas. In the case of *The Midlands* guide the most obvious example of this is Briercliffe's suggestion to use the Great North Road and sections of the A1, A5 and A10 to cycle north out of London towards the Midlands. He makes no mention of the unsuitability of these roads for the cyclist because of the volume of traffic or even the need to avoid the M25 (or the M5, M6 and M42 motorway network around Birmingham) because in 1950 Britain's motorway network was still very much on the drawing board. In 1946 the first map was published showing the planned motorway system, including lines that became the M1, M4, M5, M6, M62 and M18 (there was also a circle around London that would eventually become the M25). In the same year, the Government also announced an 80% expansion of the trunk-road system, adding an extra 3,500 miles to the network. A series of trunk-road improvements took place throughout the 1950s, a decade which ended with the opening of the M1 in November 1959.

This gradual increase in Britain's highway capacity coincided with the growth in car ownership and use. The Department for Transport has recorded levels of use of the various types of transport (in annual billion vehicle kms) every year since 1949. Cycling has declined rapidly since the 1950s from a high of 24 billion vehicle kms in 1949 to around 5 billion vehicle kms in 2010. In the same 61-year period, car usage has risen from just over 20 billion vehicle kms in 1949 to almost 400 billion vehicle kms by 2010. Against this backdrop, it is little wonder that the road conditions Briercliffe describes at the end of the 1940s seem to bear so little relationship to what would be found if you tried cycle touring on Britain's trunk-road network today.

In addition to this massive increase in highway capacity and traffic levels, Britain experienced significant house building in the post-war years, leading to the expansion of major urban conurbations as well as some of our smaller towns and cities. There are many reminders of the obvious changes that have occurred since the 1940s in Briercliffe's description of the places he visited on his journeys. Briercliffe's route from London towards the Midlands involved passing through Stevenage, which was designated a New Town by the government in the 1946 New Towns Act. The town was transformed, swelling from around 6,000 inhabitants to a population of over 80,000. The 1946 New Towns Act resulted in similar levels of development in such places as Bracknell, Crawley, Hemel Hempstead, Basildon and Harlow. A second wave of new-town building followed in the 1960s, including more towns situated within the area defined by Briercliffe as the 'Midlands' region, the most significant of these being at Runcorn and Telford, with the grandest project at Milton Keynes, which was designated in January 1967.

You might wonder whether, in the face of so much housing development, road building and traffic growth since 1950, if any of the UK that Briercliffe discovered on his journeys still exists. It is therefore reassuring to find that so much of the distinctive character of Briercliffe's Britain can still be discovered by the cycle tourist. An obvious example of this within the *Central England* guide is the wonderful cycling that can be found in the Peak District. This area is one of the 10 National Parks that were designated by Government in 1949. In the period since this legislation, strict planning controls have limited the amount of development so that much of the varied landscape described by Briercliffe remains as it was in the 1940s. The last sixty years represents a mere blink of an eye in comparison to the millions of years over which the 'geological foundation' of the Peak District was formed. The underlying limestone and millstone grit rock which dominates the area has created a landscape that has changed very little since Briercliffe's time. The rock types have a significant impact on the ecology of the area and these variations can still be viewed when cycling in areas such as the Upper Derwent Valley. It includes the series of reservoirs along the valley, only two of which (Howden and Derwent) were built by the time Harold wrote his guide book. The Derwent Reservoir, completed in 1916, had been used during World War II as the Dambusters Squadron prepared for their dramatic raids on German dams. Today, the series of reservoirs and their surrounds have been developed for tranquil recreational uses, including fishing as well as a network of paths for walking and cycling.

The network of such paths is now quite extensive throughout the Peak District. While many of the on-road routes that Briercliffe mentions have become much more trafficked and unsuitable for cyclists, quieter segregated cycle paths are now more available than they were in the 1940s. Much use has been made of the unused old railway lines. Some 4,000 miles of railway branch line was shut during 'Beeching's Axe' of the 1960s. In the last few decades some of these old railway routes have been converted to form excellent paths for cyclists and pedestrians. As cycle routes they have become a much-valued facility, free from the hazards of fast-moving motor vehicles and are generally very flat, not exceeding a gradient of more than about 1 in 20. So while Briercliffe might have recommended using sections of what have become busy A roads (such as the A6 to leave Bakewell) today's reader would be well advised to check the alternative modern-day Sustrans routes (identified at the end of each chapter). A good example of such a route is the very popular Tissington Trail, which follows the line of the old railway tracks between Ashbourne and Buxton. There are similar converted railway paths throughout the Peak District, including the Sett Valley Trail, Monsal Trail, Manifold and Hamps Trail, Longendale Trail and the High Peak Trail.

Another major change in the Peak District, and elsewhere in Britain, is the availability of Youth Hostel accommodation. Briercliffe mentions the suitability of Whitemeadows, Langsett and Rudyard Lake Youth Hostels as providing a base for exploring the area. However, these hostels (along with many others mentioned throughout Briercliffe's guides) were among the casualties of the hostel-closure programme. This would not have been anticipated by Briercliffe back in the late 1940s when membership of the Youth Hostel Association (YHA) was heading towards its peak. At the start of the 1950s there were 303 youth hostels and over 200,000 YHA members. Increased availability of holidays abroad and changes in the level of walking and hiking resulted in a gradual fall in demand for YHA accommodation. This led to closures and a modernisation programme with the emphasis on providing better youth-hostel facilities in towns and cities. Around 100 of the hostels (particularly those in more remote rural areas) were closed. Thankfully, some of the hostels mentioned by Briercliffe remain open. These include the impressive Ilam Hall Youth Hostel (page 22), which continues to provide an excellent base for exploring the area.

Moving beyond the confines of the Peak District, many of the routes that Briercliffe identifies in his journeys around Central England are still perfectly suitable for the keen touring cyclist. Much of the landscape between the west side of the Birmingham conurbation and the Welsh borders retains something of the quiet remoteness that Briercliffe was so keen to praise. This is particularly the case in the area to the west of the Wyre Forest, crossing back and forth between the counties of Herefordshire and Shropshire and around Wenclock Edge and Corvedale. Further to the north, the landscape between Wolverhampton and Shrewsbury has changed much more dramatically since the 1960s with the introduction of the M54 motorway and the rapid development of Telford. The area to the south west, through the Welsh Marches, seems to have been a particular favourite of Briercliffe's. He describes the cycle route from Shrewsbury to Hereford as benefiting from 'one of the finest and fastest main roads in the country.' He identifies Church Stretton and Ludlow as particular highlights along the route and is keen to emphasise the wonderful scenery that can be viewed from locations such as Dinmore Hill near Leominster. Sixty years on, Ludlow is still dominated by its Castle, dating back to Norman times and Church Stretton still retains its charm created by the backdrop of the Stretton Hills and Long Mynd. Unfortunately, the A49 between Shrewsbury and Hereford is no longer the attractive cycling route that Briercliffe once described, undergoing a series of upgrades that now present sections of dual carriageway and much higher flows of fast moving traffic. Travelling further south towards Monmouth, Briercliffe continues to emphasise the beauty of the scenery along the route. His description of the views of Symonds Yat is very much in keeping with today's accounts of this popular spot. Certainly this remains an attractive location for cyclists and can now best be experienced using the recommended Sustrans route.

A vast area was covered by Briercliffe in what he called his 'Midlands' guide. He describes routes out of London, heading north and east towards Lincolnshire and even to the Norfolk coast. He also sets out an extensive network of routes across the core of Central England, linking places with historic interest such as Stratford-upon-Avon, Worcester and Malvern. It is noticeable that the roads between towns and cities seem to have changed more than the description of the towns themselves. The latest designated Sustrans routes described at the end of each chapter are therefore an invaluable tool in helping today's cyclist to rediscover the extent to which the essential character of these towns and the wider countryside has remained intact over the course of the last 60 years.

Mark Jarman
2012

Whatever the Mileage

-the Super Club will get you there

The Super Club (illustrated below) is a superb example of how completely Elswick and Hopper cycles have returned to traditional standards. Many complimentary letters are continually being received from enthusiastic owners praising the beautiful finish of our cycles. Excellent though our models now are we are persistently and painstakingly devoting all our technical skill to even greater progress in design.

Elswick & Hopper Cycles

**ELSWICK HOPPER CYCLE & MOTOR CO. LTD.,
BARTON-ON-HUMBER, LINCOLNSHIRE**

PREFACE

FOR the first time in this series of guides I deal in this book with an area which lacks the attraction of a coast. The guides dealing with Northern England, Wales, the Scottish Highlands and South-West England all featured long stretches of seashore, and in them there was constant reference to the sea.

In the Midlands there are no adequate topographical compensations for the absence of the ocean. This book is comprehensive enough to reveal the interest of the Severn Estuary and of the estuaries of the River Dee and River Mersey, but their glories are milder than those of, say, the Mawddach or Loch Torridon.

Nevertheless, the Midlands have their attractions in plenty for the tourist. But before I go any farther, I had better define the area—and it is a big one—covered by this guide.

"Northern England" reached down as far as the River Mersey and the course of its tributary, the Etherow, at Woodhead, and took in the district north of the Barnsley-Doncaster road. All south of that line, right down to the northern edge of the Cotswolds, comes into this volume.

"Wales" took in all the country—including a large slice of England—west of the line Chester-Whitchurch-Ludlow-Hereford-Monmouth-Newport. There lies the westerly boundary of this book. On the east, the course of the Great North Road southwards forms the boundary from Doncaster, past Bawtry, Retford, Newark, Grantham, Stamford, Norman Cross, Alconbury Hill, and then along the *old* North Road by Huntingdon, Royston, Ware and Hoddesdon to the Thames again at London Bridge.

"The Midlands," then, for the purposes of this guide, constitutes a far-flung region. Classification of a series of guides which will eventually cover the entire British Isles is not easy, and because of the relatively restricted areas covering adjacent touring districts, "the Midlands" have been extended in size and importance.

I must admit at once that for the cyclist and walker Central England has a smaller appeal than the Lake District, the Yorkshire Dales and Coast, North and Mid Wales and the Scottish Highlands. It is primarily given over by the cyclist to day trips, weekends and short holidays such as Easter, Whitsun and Christmas.

Only the Peak District, duly extended to bring in East Cheshire and North Staffordshire, provides sufficient interest for a week or a fortnight's tour. But the cyclist who cares to link up—as he can very easily—short tours of Shakespeare's Country, the Malverns, the lower Wye Valley and the Forest of Dean, as given in their respective chapters, will find that he has presented himself with one of the most varied and unusual holidays that he will find south of the Scottish Border, east of Wales and north of Bridgwater.

Finally, I should like to thank my cycling friends who have helped me with their advice on the Midlands, notably E. R. Forscutt, of Kettering, and Charles Fearnley, the health expert. Their knowledge of a few obscure corners was freely offered and gratefully accepted.

HAROLD BRIERCLIFFE.

Letchworth, Herts.

December, 1948.

CHAPTER I

THE PEAK DISTRICT

INTRODUCTION

THE Peak District is not large and it is not remote. Moreover, it is hemmed in by a ring of manufacturing towns and cities. The cyclist who goes there should not expect to find himself amidst the solitudes that are to be found in the more northerly parts of the Pennine Chain.

It follows, therefore, that the Peak District calls for leisurely and patient exploration. Any rider who goes in for mile-eating will quickly find himself in Clay Cross or in Hanley or Ancoats—hardly halts for the tourist.

Because of its geological foundation, the Peak—here signifying North Derbyshire, East Cheshire, East Staffordshire, and even part of Lancashire and Yorkshire—has great variety within a limited compass. The core of the district, from Chapel-en-le-Frith and Castleton southwards to near Ashbourne, is chiefly limestone, that fantastic rock which gives deep gorges—old caverns with their roofs fallen in; weird, isolated hills, as near Longnor; and miles of dull, uninspiring upland.

This limestone core is flanked by millstone grit, a harder, more durable, relative of sandstone. The grit is warmer altogether, and makes for impressive "edges" and more romantic scenery. The upper Derwent Valley, near Grindleford Bridge, forms part of the dividing line between the two rocks. It is a stimulating experience to stand on the hills north of Eyam and look westward across the limestone upland, undulating in smooth, stone-walled surges, and then to turn eastwards and gaze across the trough formed by the Derwent and the steep castellations of the gritstone on the far side of the valley.

The Midland gritstone does not achieve its most outstanding scenic phase in Derbyshire at all. This honour is reserved for the steep little gorges and their plunging streams that abound on and around the River Dane, near Swithamley. The river thereabouts separates Cheshire from Staffordshire. In this district, too, are the remarkable pieces of natural statuary formed by The Roaches and Hen Cloud. These eroded rock shapes lie just west of the Leek-Buxton road.

"The Peak," or Kinder Scout, consists of a plateau over 2,000 ft. high, and of irregular shape. It is about 1½ miles by 4½ miles, and in composition is sterile bog overlaying millstone grit. The plateau is scored in all directions by deep and treacherous watercourses, each one like its neighbour, all full of pitfalls to the unwary, and literally deadly in mist or fog. There are few acknowledged footpaths across Kinder Scout, and grouse and keepers have the wilderness nearly to themselves. From time to time daring parties and individuals have braved the bogs, the weather and the keepers and have been up the hill. In the 1930s a "mass trespass" took place which led to arrests and to imprisonment.

The most impressive features of Kinder Scout, however, are the edges which buttress the summit bogs. These are steep gritstone faces reaching down boldly from the plateau towards the valleys. One striking face of this kind is Fairbrook Naze, noticeable from the public footpath along Ashop Clough, between Hayfield and the Snake Inn. The grandest piece of scenery on Kinder Scout, however, is Kinder Downfall. This is a mere trickle in summer and autumn, but in winter the stream feeding the fall becomes a torrent, spreading out in a fan across the gritstone and falling hundreds of feet into the valley below.

Perhaps no county in England has so much to show in natural phenomena as Derbyshire. Castleton has a glut of caverns and two impressive limestone gorges in The Winnats and Cave Dale. In the nearby limestone, too, there are the "bottomless" Eldon Hole and the Bagshaw Cavern at Bradshaw. Mam Tor, or the "Shivering Mountain," dominates the head of the Hope Valley, west of Castleton, and its shaley face does "shiver" in the right conditions.

There are other caves, too, at Buxton, while at Matlock there are more commercialized "wonders."

Accommodation in the Peak District is now getting back slowly towards the standards which prevailed before the war. More and more of the farms and smaller houses are offering bed and breakfast and meals.

The Youth Hostels Association has covered the Peak District with some 25 hostels. These vary in capacity and in kind—there is quite a difference between the large hostels, such as Hartington Hall or Ilam Hall, and the more modest Windgather.

The camper who shuns the larger sites in the vicinity of such places as Hayfield, Castleton and Baslow and takes himself to the hill farms will find that Derbyshire has plenty to offer in the way of rural surroundings, sheltered pitches and ample water supply and dairy produce.

The main roads of the Peak District are consistently good. Tarred limestone makes a hard, durable and non-skid surface, although the untarred limestone by-roads can be quite "tacky" after rain. Gritstone by-roads dry quickly and in rain are firm and non-skid.

APPROACHES

Unlike the more distant touring grounds, the central situation of the Peak District enables the cyclist from most of the large cities and towns south of the line Preston-Hull to reach at least the fringes of the district in a day's riding. Derby, for instance, is only 126 miles from London by the direct route through Leicester. A strong rider could do this distance fairly comfortably in a long day.

Some of the alternative road routes between London and the Midlands are given in the chapter headed "Northwards from London." The handiest direct way runs through Barnet, Hatfield, Welwyn, Codicote, Hitchin, Bedford, Rushden, Kettering, Market Harborough, Leicester and so into Derby.

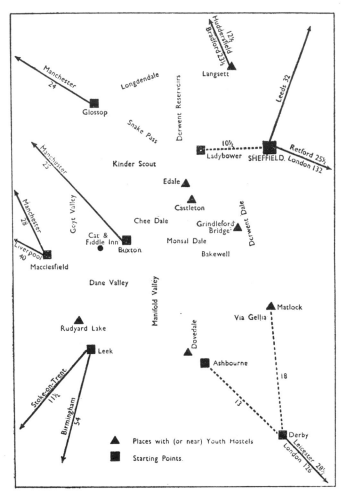

Approaches to the Peak District

(not to scale)

The following tour starts and finishes at Derby because of that town's situation on the south side of the Peak District. It is, therefore, closest to London and to Birmingham. Derby has little to detain the tourist.

The Manchester cyclist may join the round at Glossop, which he can reach by way of the indifferent road through Denton, Hyde and Mottram Cutting.

From Liverpool the handiest route lies through Warrington, Knutsford, Macclesfield and Sutton, joining the tour at Danebridge.

For the Potteries rider, the junction with the tour can be best made by going through Leek to Upper Hulme, at the foot of the Roaches.

A sporting entry into the Peak District for riders from Leeds and Bradford lies across the moors to the Flouch Inn, where the roads from Manchester to Barnsley and from Huddersfield to Sheffield cross. Southwards from Langsett (itself south-east of the Flouch Inn) a moorland lane rambles and falls, tips and dips, past Upper Midhope, Ewden and the Strines Inn to the Sheffield-Manchester road above the Ashopton Reservoir. By going right and descending to the Reservoir, the main route can be joined. There are convenient youth hostels close to this picturesque entrance to Peakland, at Fulshaw Cross (not far from Langsett) and at Ewden village, east of the route from the Flouch Inn.

From Sheffield, nearest of all cities to the Peak District, the route can be joined at the Ashopton Reservoir and continued southward from there.

Railway routes to the Peak District are varied. From London, Bristol and the south-west and from Birmingham, the obvious jumping-off point is Derby, served by excellent express services.

Derby is also served by expresses from Bradford, Leeds, Edinburgh and Glasgow. These trains are either direct or nearly so. Similarly, Sheffield is on main lines from these northern cities.

While I recommend Derby as the principal starting-point, a good deal can be said for Sheffield. The city's roads are far better than they were, and the climbs into Peakland, running west and south-west, are in their way perhaps as spectacular entrances as any. There is, first, a steady climb on fair surfaces through Sheffield's not unlovely western suburbs. Then the open moorland is gained, with fewer houses and many stone walls. At the summit level the eye looks out over a lively panorama of moor and hill. Lower down the roads pass close to the "edges," and again there are views, this time of the Derwent in its green dale. After that, Peakland lies before the tourist, his merely for the cycling.

Besides the routes to Sheffield already outlined, there are those of the former L.N.E.R. My own favourite railway journey to Sheffield commences at Marylebone, London. This line is not as busy as the one from St. Pancras, and over it at least two crack trains pass daily in both directions. These are comfortable and fast.

Another approach over the former L.N.E.R. starts at King's Cross. A change is needed at Retford for Sheffield by this route, however.

A futher excellent cross-country service for the rider, commencing at Sheffield, is formed by the expresses running from Newcastle to the south coast by way of York, Sheffield, Banbury, Oxford and Swindon.

Manchester and Liverpool cyclists are perhaps too near the Peak District to seek railway lifts there, but riders from both cities who require rail assistance should not neglect the service to Penistone on the Sheffield line.

Nottingham and Eastern Counties cyclists could join the route at Derby.

I need only repeat now that the first tour as written starts and finishes at Derby. Halting-places are given on that understanding. On the other hand, riders who choose to start elsewhere will find little trouble in adapting the tour to their own requirements.

The tour is drafted on the assumption that Derby is left not later than 3 p.m.

ROUND OF THE PEAK DISTRICT
A 13-day Tour
(Derby to Derby—230 miles)

Leave **Derby** (Art Gallery) by way of Friargate and Ashbourne Road. More details of Derby are given on pages 61 62.

From the London Midland Region station at Derby, Friatgate may be reached by way of Midland Road, London Road and St. Peters Street, turning left out of the latter into Victoria Street and Wardwick for Friargate.

Riders approaching the town from London and Leicester need not enter the congested central part of Derby, but can go left some three miles south of the town along a by-pass which reaches the Ashbourne road some six miles farther on. The shortest way is through the town, however, particularly if the tourist is making for Matlock or returning from that resort.

The Ashbourne Road, formerly one of the main roads between London and Manchester, and used by Prince Charles Edward Stuart during his advance on Derby in 1745, heads in a north-westerly direction and gradually climbs into pastoral country past Mackworth, Kirk Langley and Brailsford, beyond which, on the left, are the grounds of Osmaston Park. A steep hill leads down into the streets of **Ashbourne** (13 miles from Derby), the graceful spire of its church being a prominent feature. A description of the town appears on page 57.

Ashbourne or its vicinity is recommended for the first night's halt. There is a selection of accommodation in the town, while the tourist seeking quieter quarters will find them in one of the several villages a few miles to the north: Tissington, Parwich and Brassington notably.

There is a good choice of youth-hostel accommodation within easy reach of Ashbourne, at Ilam Hall (90 beds), Whitemeadows (60 beds) and Brassington (12 beds). The Ashbourne district is recommended for a stay of at least two nights, the object being to visit Dovedale, four miles north. A secondary excursion, involving a third night's stay (see page 28) might be to the romantic Churnet Valley, near Alton Towers.

Ilam Hall, over five miles north of Ashbourne, is the closest youth hostel to the foot of Dovedale, and there is also bed-and-breakfast accommodation nearby.

———————

From Ashbourne, the route to the foot of Dovedale lies, first, along the Buxton road, which goes northward steeply from the Market Place. A mile out of the town the way is leftwards, crossing a stream and going under the Ashbourne-Buxton railway. Ahead rises the first "peak," the conical hill called Thorpe Cloud (942 ft.), the green sentinel at the south end of Dovedale.

Three miles from Ashbourne, a left fork should be taken past the village of Thorpe, and downhill to a bridge across the River Dove, not far from the Izaak Walton Hotel. Bicycles should be left in safe custody in this area. The Hotel is about 4½ miles from Ashbourne.

About three-quarters of a mile ahead, also on the west (Staffordshire) bank of the Dove, is the village of Ilam. This is a "model village" built in a most picturesque style. **Ilam Hall Youth Hostel**, of Elizabethan architecture, lies to the south-west in its own grounds. The hall was erected in the 1800s, despite its architectural style and ancient appearance. Nearby the River Manifold bubbles up out of the earth after a subterranean course of several miles. Hostellers will, of course, leave their bicycles at Ilam Hall if staying there overnight.

A full day could be spent in exploring **Dovedale** afoot. Food should be carried, although one or two of the cottages at Mill Dale, 3 miles northward and at the end of "Dovedale" proper, provide light meals.

The section of the valley of the River Dove, which has rightly acquired a wide reputation for its scenery, extends for nearly three miles northwards from the Stepping Stones, at the foot of the dale, to Dove Holes, just south of the narrow bridge at Mill Dale.

It might be as well at this point to warn intending visitors that on Bank Holiday weekends and at other popular holiday times the amount of solitude in Dovedale proper is very small indeed.

The path up Dovedale keeps to the Derbyshire, or east, side of the valley. The west side, wholly in Staffordshire, is not followed by any continuous path. The approach from Ilam or from the Izaac

Walton Hotel first runs in a north-easterly direction, and the scenery begins at the Stepping Stones, which are crossed to the Derbyshire bank below the steep sides of Thorpe Cloud.

Dewpond under
THORPE CLOUD

Dovedale is neither magnificent nor grand in the sense that Glencoe or the Pass of Llanberis are. It is, however, perhaps the happiest combination of rock, woodland and water in the British Isles. Throughout the distance between the Stepping Stones and the Dove Holes the scenery remains consistently beautiful.

From the Stepping Stones the riverside track climbs to Sharplow Point, one of the best viewpoints in the dale. The Dove is here broken up by little weirs, and pressing closely on both banks are trees: ash, hawthorn and hazel. On the Staffordshire side can be seen the limestone crags called the Twelve Apostles. Sharplow Point lies a little to the left of the path, and can be readily reached. It is a bare rock above an angle in the stream, and from it there are commanding views up and down the valley. From this point Thorpe Cloud can be seen rising sharply in the south. Towards the north Dovedale contracts into a gorge between perpendicular cliffs.

Continuing, Tissington Spires, a series of pinnacles, can be noticed on the right-hand side. Soon the track regains the waterside, and at a fork the tourist can either climb rightwards to Reynard's

Cave or keep near the stream. It is worthwhile ascending to the Cave for the views given en route of the narrowest part of Dovedale.

Back by the stream, the valley contracts to its narrowest. On the Staffordshire side there is no foothold at all, and even on the Derbyshire bank the path has to keep to a slender causeway between the Dove and the rocks. The causeway is under water at times of flood.

This is perhaps the most beautiful part of Dovedale. The trees contrast sharply with the silvery stream. Ahead is a rock—on the Derbyshire side—called the Lion's Head. On the left is Ilam Rock. A little ahead, on the right, are the Dove Holes, two wide and shallow caves.

The going is more commonplace until the Dove has to be crossed by the narrow pack-horse bridge, picturesquely placed amongst foliage, which gives access to the road and the few cottages of **Mill Dale**.

It should be pointed out that nearly the whole of Dovedale and much of the valley above Mill Dale belongs to the National Trust.

Those wishing to return directly to Ashbourne or Ilam Hall could take lunch at Mill Dale, and then follow the road north-eastwards to Lode Mill, there commencing the climb of a subsidiary dale which goes east. Some way up this a steep little side road climbs leftwards through a grove and emerges on the Buxton-Ashbourne main highway. Directly opposite lies Alsop-en-le-Dale Station. From this point the less energetic could take train back to Thorpe Cloud Station (for Ilam Hall) or Ashbourne. Unfortunately, the train times are not altogether convenient. The only two suitable services from Alsop are at 11.17 a.m. and 6.33 p.m.

Those wishing to walk back to Ilam or Ashbourne will find that about half a mile south of the station a high-level lane leaves the main Ashbourne road and eventually rejoins the lane from Ilam to Ashbourne at a crossroads east of Thorpe village.

Energetic walkers might care to continue the walk from Mill Dale through **Wolfscote Dale** and **Beresford Dale** to Hartington, a further 5 miles of walking.

At Lode Mill a path should be taken on the east side of the Dove.

This northerly extension of the valley of the Dove is much quieter than the popular stretch between Thorpe Cloud and the Dove Holes and at first hardly as pretty.

The path is easily followed, however. The dale is still deep, a limestone cleft winding like a bare corridor through the limestone. Trees are fewer than farther south.

At about four miles from Mill Dale a cart track crosses the river by a bridge, and for a few hundred yards the Staffordshire side is followed. Entering Beresford Dale, the tourist finds himself in one of the finest reaches of the valley. Steep limestone crags, covered in part by trees, enclose the dale. The Pike Pool, towards the northern end, should be noticed. Here, a sharp pointed rock rises from the middle of the stream. The path returns to the Derbyshire bank, and soon, on the other side, can be seen the Fishing House, a one-roomed affair with a pointed roof. It was associated with Isaac Walton, author of *The Compleat Angler*.

After the brief beauty of Beresford Dale, the tourist can cross the meadows to the village of **Hartington**, which lies off the main roads and is a picturesque place. Hartington Hall Youth Hostel stands to the east of the village on high ground.

Hartington Station, for the evening train (6.25 p.m.) to Thorpe Cloud (for Ilam Hall) and Ashbourne, lies 3 miles east.

Ashbourne, or Ilam Hall, or Whitemeadows Youth Hostels make good starting-points for a further excursion, this time by bicycle.

The villages, moors, dales and antiquities lying inside the rectangle formed by Ashbourne, Parsley Hay Station (on the Buxton line), Great Rowsley and Wirksworth compose a touring ground which can be reached conveniently from Ashbourne, although some of the attractions along its northern and eastern borders lie also within the orbits of tourlets from Buxton, Bakewell or Matlock.

Ashbourne is indicated as the starting-point, but the hosteller staying at Ilam Hall can link up with the route quite easily by going eastward from the hostel by Thorpe and by turning left just before Thorpe Cloud Station, and reaching the Tissington crossroads (see below) on the Ashbourne-Buxton main road.

The non-hostelling tourist should travel northward towards Buxton from Ashbourne, in 3½ miles reaching the Tissington crossroads. Here the way is rightward into the lovely Derbyshire village of **Tissington** (4 miles from Ashbourne). This is one of the county's loveliest villages, a delightful place with a church on a knoll and an Elizabethan hall, as well as much charming domestic architecture. The chief fame of Tissington, however, lies around its wells. Until the 1939-45 war the annual well-dressing at Tissington on Ascension Day was an established local custom. Five wells in the village were "dressed" by flower petals, mosses and other constituents into mosaics of Biblical scenes superimposed on clay.

From the east end of Tissington a pleasant hill road runs to the Ashbourne-Bakewell main road, where the way is leftward. In about three miles from Tissington a lane strikes leftward off the main road and makes for Parwich. In the triangle of the two thoroughfares stands, on the left, the large and pleasant youth hostel of **Whitemeadows**, a convenient alternative to Ilam Hall for hostellers.

Parwich (8 miles from Ashbourne by this route) is a large village snugly placed at the southern side of a series of rounded green hills. There are possibilities here of bed-and-breakfast accommodation.

From Parwich the lane heading north-westward by Parwich Moor should be taken. This joins the Ashbourne-Buxton main road a little south of the 12th milestone from Buxton (11 miles from Ashbourne by this route). The main road should be followed northward next, past the old coaching haunt of the **Newhaven Inn**, where the way is leftward, still towards Buxton.

A few hundred yards short of the 8th milestone from Buxton, with Parsley Hall Station in a hollow on the left, a right fork should be taken. A short way along this a further right turn must be taken, towards the east. A mile down this secondary road the bicycle should be abandoned while **Arbor Low**, situated a short way south, is sought out.

Arbor Low is a stone circle, sometimes called, without much justification, "the Stonehenge of the Midlands." It consists of 40 stones, some of them 12 ft. in length, but all lying flat within a ditch and an earthwork.

Regaining the road again, the way awheel leads along The Long Rake. Although several turns go rightwards, the route to follow descends leftwards throughout to the foot of the slope at

Conksbury Bridge (20), where the River Lathkill is met. The bridge is situated at one of the prettiest parts of the short but most romantic River Lathkill. Here the thorough tourist should halt awhile to assimilate the beauty of the scene: a clear stream running through woodlands between graceful green slopes. The valley can be explored afoot.

Beyond the bridge a steady rise of a mile leads to an upland road junction where the way is leftwards to the village of **Over Haddon** (22), a pretty halting-place perched high above Lathkill Dale on its north side. From Over Haddon, on its hill, a lane leads northward over the moorlands, and then descends, after a right turn, into **Bakewell** (24), perhaps the most pleasant of all the Derbyshire resorts, and one that is admirably situated as a centre. A full description of the town appears on page 58.

From Bakewell the main road leading south-west should be taken. This is A6, the London–Carlisle road, and for nearly three miles the route runs along it through gracious valley scenery. In 2 miles, on the left-hand side, **Haddon Hall** may be glimpsed through the trees. The hall lies on the far bank of the River Wye, across a bridge. The hall is not shown to visitors, as it is the residence of the Duke of Rutland. It is a romantic place, gradually put together over the centuries, and never disturbed by siege. The public imagination links it with the story of the elopement of Dorothy Vernon and Sir John Manners at the end of the 16th century.

About 900 yds. beyond the entrance to the hall a side road goes rightwards and gently ascends with the River Lathkill for another mile.

At the next fork it is worthwhile going rightwards for another 1½ miles with the River Lathkill by the pretty riverside village of Alport into **Youlgreave**, a fascinating small town with a fine church which includes a conspicuous tower.

The main route, however, turns left towards the south and traces a narrowing tributary dale which runs between sandstone crests, some amidst trees. Notable on the right is Cratcliffe Wood, and a little farther on stretches Robin Hood's Stride, a remarkable collection of rocks from which there is a splendid view over the upland valley traversed by the road.

The road which was entered below Alport—A524—climbs

beyond Robin Hood's Stride to higher ground, and reaches a crossroads between Elton (rightward) and Winster (leftward). At **Elton** there is a small, simple youth hostel at Elton Old Hall. The thorough tourist should eschew the direct course of A524 and turn left into the old-fashioned townlet of **Winster** (31). The place is built on a slope and has an old market hall.

Out of Winster a lane runs south-west and soon rejoins A524. A tun across bare upland follows, and then the highway begins to drop steadily—a fine freewheel—to the few buildings of Grange Mill, where the head of the **Via Gellia** valley (see page 64) is crossed. There follows a steady climb lasting 1½ miles, and then the High Peak Railway is crossed. As the road begins to drop down a limestone valley the attractive pile of Brassington Rocks can be seen on the right (**Brassington**, on the left, has a simple youth hostel, holding 12).

Towards the foot of the next descent, a little beyond the turn rightward for Parwich, a glimpse of **Whitemeadows Youth Hostel** may be seen. The highway next traces the course of the charming Bradbourne Brook to where road and stream meet the Buxton-Ashbourne highway, about two miles north of the latter town.

This round of 43 miles only is so full of interest that the whole of a long summer's day could be spent on it.

The tourist with plenty of time, or the weekender intent on seeing some of the most romantic valley scenery in Staffordshire, should remember the attractions of the **Churnet Valley**. The Rivet Chutnet in its course between Oakamoor and Denstone follows a narrow gorge between wooded hills. The stream itself is sullied by industrial effluvia from higher up its course, and after a dry summer is any colour but peat-brown or limestone grey. The best part of the Churnet Valley can be reached quite readily in an out-and-home day run from Ashbourne or one of the nearby youth hostels.

It will be seen from the foregoing descriptions that the Ashbourne district (and the youth hostels to the north and west) provides an excellent base from which to explore the valley scenery at the south end of the Peak District. Its proximity to the large Midland cities marks it out as a region for exploration at Easter or Whitsuntide, or for any short tour. Even the

London cyclist, by hard riding or with train assistance, could make a fine four-day holiday out of a base in the Ashbourne district, using the preceding section of this guide as a plan.

Leaving Ashbourne and resuming the main tour, the route first goes by Thorpe Village to Ilam, crossing the River Dove just short of the latter (this route is described fuller on page 22). A right turn near the bridge in Ilam (the river on the left is the Manifold, which will be appearing [or disappearing] time and time again in the next few paragraphs), and a further rightward bend at a subsequent fork takes the tourist northward to open land between the valleys of the Dove and the Manifold. This is typical limestone hill country— consisting of waves of rolling fields broken by innumerable white walls. Occasionally a shallow, waterless dale goes right or left to meet the Dove or the Manifold valleys.

Hopedale (21 miles from Derby, 8 from Ashbourne) is a crossroads village (in Staffordshire), where it may be possible to get a meal. The way is leftward here. In a few yards the through lane goes rightward towards Wetton, but the route lies straight on. This rough by-lane drops steeply towards the River Manifold, taking a sharp left turn down a very sharp final section to a farm road on the north-east bank of the bed of the. stream.

The **River Manifold** is one of the most curious in England. Together with the course of its tributary, the River Hamps, which joins it from the south opposite the by-road entrance from Hopedale, most of the course of the Manifold between Wetton Mill and the grounds of Ilam Hall is dry in a normal summer. The Manifold is then coy, and, with the Hamps, flows underground. Just east, or left, of where the Hopedale by-road meets the stream bed stands **Beeston Tor**, a noble hill.

The route of a former line of light railway between Waterhouses (on the Ashbourne-Leek main road) and Hulme End (on the Hartington-Cheadle [Staffs] road) has now been converted into a footpath. Cycling is forbidden along this level track, but it is quite possible to wheel a bicycle along it. The scenery, while inferior to that of the best of Dovedale, deserves the closer attention possible when walking.

The former railway route lies on the west side of the river, and can be reached by Weag's Bridge. The track winds northward through the best part of the valley, now and then passing hillside plantations and isolated copses. The valley is narrow and there is not much room for woodlands or for farm buildings.

The absence of water in this part of the valley has troubled the local dairy farmers, too.

A mile from Weag's Bridge a great hole opens in the face of the opposite, or east, side of the valley. This is **Thor's Cave**, in the face of a large outcrop of rock. The cave is more imposing for its width and as a viewpoint than for any other interest, although during the last century British relics were found in it.

At Wetton Mill, 2 miles from Beeston Tor, the rail track can be left, the river re-crossed, and a lane on the east bank, which winds northward can be followed. On the right the hillside climbs steeply to the summit of Ecton Hill, once vigorously worked for copper. The route, improving in surface as it goes, reaches the hamlet of Hulme End, whence a short climb and fall lead to a bridge across the River Dove and into **Hartington** (29), where there is a youth hostel. More details of this large village, a useful place for lunch, appear on page 25.

The direct-lane route between Ashbourne or Ilam and Harrington continues across upland northward from Hopedale by **Alstonfield**, a large village with a church containing a pew erected by Charles Cotton, into Hulme End. The distance from Hopedale to Hartington is about 5½ miles.

The most westerly of the two lanes northward out of Hartington leads past a pond and along a lane at first lined by cottages and gardens, past Banktop, and then, in about a mile, to the side of the River Dove. Ahead now opens a bare green valley, dotted with the white of farmhouses. To the right climbs a hillside. The valley comes down from the north-west.

The hills tend to become more individual again as the route undulates on its way. The most noticeable hereabouts is Sheen Hill (1,247 ft.), which rises on the far, or Staffordshire, bank of the Dove. At the farmyard hamlet of Pilsbury the metalled road swings rightward to join (in 3½ miles) the main Ashbourne-Buxton road at Hindlow. The tourist should maintain his direction up the tranquil valley, however. Half a mile of farm road leads to **Pilsbury Castle**, a raised mound surmounted by trees lying to the left of the road and between it and the river. The route continues as a field track (with several gates), which can be ridden. This part of the Dove Valley is serene and unfrequented.

A metalled road is met again close to the white hamlet of **Crowdecote** (33), a tiny place crowding round the foot of a descent on the highway between Bakewell and Longnor. The latter lies a mile west, over a low ridge which hereabouts is all that divides the headwaters of the rivers Dove and Manifold. Out of Crowdecote the way is clear—across the Dove into Staffordshire again, and uphill for half a mile and down for the same into the little town of Longnor.

Longnor (34), although on the road from Buxton, to Cheadle (Staffs), is as quaint a place as there is in the Staffordshire Moorlands. There is a market hall and a few rambling streets and alleys that is all. It is perhaps its breezy situation on the side of a hill that makes Longnor so appealing. Everywhere there are good walks and excursions. Buxton lies less than six miles away, and there is the inevitable 'bus service. Yet Longnor survives much the same as it did 20 years ago when I first came to know it. There is refreshment here for the hungry cyclist if he needs lunch or tea. Overnight accommodation is not found so easily, but anyone seeking a quiet base for the Derbyshire and Staffordshire dales or for the rugged gritstone upland to the west could hardly do better than stay at Longnor.

CHROME HILL

31

The sojourner at Longnor planning his excursions or the tourist halting there briefly will get a splendid glimpse into the scenic possibilities of the district if he goes a mile northward along the Buxton road. A halt as the road begins to dip towards Glutton Mill will yield as rewarding a vision of limestone Derbyshire as will be found in the whole of the district. Away to the south-east, above the silvery Dove, rise the steep crags of High Wheeldon (1,384 ft., the tallest hill in the immediate district). Towards the north-east and north pile the running ridges. But all the surprises are congregated to the north-west. There stand, like Derbyshire Dolomites, on the north bank of the Dove, the striking sentinels of Hollins Hill and Chrome Hill, two fortresses wrought in spirited limestone. There is not a viewpoint in the whole of the limestone peak so sensational as this. Even the lower heights, such as nearby Parkhouse Hill, share in the general inclination to tower. Hollins Hill lies to the west of Chrome Hill, perhaps the most impressive of the two dominating piles.

The through tourist should take the Buxton road out of Longnor, pause at the point mentioned in the previous paragraph, and then continue to Glutton Mill (ahead the Buxton road proceeds through the narrow pass of Glutton Dale, well worth traversing and re-tracing to Glutton Mill—about a mile return). Immediately over the River Dove a farm road goes left. This is the continuation of the route through the little-visited fastnesses around the headwaters of the Rivers Dove and Manifold. Along this road Chrome Hill can be approached closely—it seems to grow more spectacular as it gets nearer. About half a mile from Glutton Mill the road swings to the right, leaving the River Dove and following a tributary up a green limestone gorge between Chrome Hill and Parkhouse Hill. Beyond the farm of Dowel, to the right, the road ascends the dry, shallow hollow of Dowel Dale, next climbing across High Edge to a better road and still heading towards the north-west.

Closer now, blocking the western sky, is Axe Edge. Below its long wall, in hollows to the left, are the springs and hollows which form the nurturing ground of the Rivers Dove and Manifold. The narrowing clough on the left seems to have as strong a claim as any to be the source of the Dove; but the springs of both rivers are generally given as quite close to the main Buxton-Leek road, which runs along the eastern crest of Axe Edge.

The minor road which has been followed joins the main Axe Edge road about 2½ miles south of Buxton at a height of about 1,500 ft. above sea level.

Directly opposite, an unfenced secondary road curls round towards the south-east, passing old quarries and then rising and falling over a great spread of moorland—passing the remains of a coal pit—before meeting the Buxton-Macclesfield road 3½ miles west of Buxton, close to the point where the Buxton-Congleton road breaks away from the Macclesfield highway. A further second-class road slips away towards the north, down to the few houses at Moss House and onwards to Goyt's Bridge (see page 41). Riders anxious to cross the Cat and Fiddle moors for Macclesfield, along the Buxton-Macclesfield highway, should take the obvious main road. In 1½ miles of up-and-down road—mostly up—"The Cat" is reached. The inn is the second highest in England, and it stands at an altitude of 1,690 ft. The origin of the name has been the subject of much conjecture, the most reasonable speculation being that it is a corruption of the name of Caton Fidele, the faithful governor of Calais.

From "The Cat" the views are immense rather than impressive. The northern part of the Peak District, including Kinder Scout, can be seen beyond the long valley of the River Goyt. To the south the shapeliest hill is Shutlings Low, a height which seems quite nearby. Farther to the south-west the crest of Bosley Cloud may be observed, backed by the smoke of the Potteries. In the west, beyond the coils of the road descending into Macclesfield, rises the little wave of Alderley Edge amidst the green sea of the Cheshire Plain. Distant atolls are the Peckforton Hills and the hill crowned by Beeston Castle (see page 79). Beyond them, Moel Fammau, in North Wales, may be discerned. The estuaries of the Mersey and the Dee are to be seen, but clear weather and the sharpest of eyesight are required to pick out Snowdon and the Glyders and the Shropshire Wrekin.

The descent into Macclesfield is more or less continuous for 7 miles. The road is well engineered, not becoming really steep until the streets of the Cheshire town itself are reached. The swirlings and twistings of the higher sections delight the free-wheeling enthusiast. From Buxton to Macclesfield via the Cat and Fiddle road is 12 miles.

On the main route, the Buxton-Leek road, high up on the eastern flanks of Axe Edge, should be followed. On the left the land shelves sharply into the bowl which contains the infant Dove and Manifold and their tributaries. The many criss-crossing walls remind the traveller that the bowl is a busy one, with sheep and cattle farming as the main occupation of its people. On the right rise barren moorlands. Just before the fourth milestone from Buxton a stream on the left bears the name of Dovehead, while a little farther on, near the Travellers' Rest Inn, at **Flash Bar**, the Manifold has its source. The inn is 1,534 ft, above sea level and the third highest in England.

There is an acute rightward bend at the inn, and about 600 yds. ahead there is a fork on the right leading into the village of Flash. This is the way to go.

The main road to Leek runs straight on, towards the south, and it continues as one of the most striking of scenic switchbacks in the whole of England. Its course is not far at first from the division of the limestone (to the east, or left) and the gritstone (to the west). In such a geological setting, drama can be expected. As the road begins to descend, a vast prospect of lonely valley and billowing upland opens to the left. At the Royal Cottage Inn a lane goes left to form a direct route to Longnor, while a little ahead another heads first east and then south along the long curving ridge called Morridge, a barrier seen to the east throughout the remaining part of the run into Leek. It is to the west, however, that the real sights are to be found. Across a dark furrow of stony upland, the battlements of the Roaches, a long spiky ridge may be seen (see also page 39). The falling road, however, leaves little time for study, and very soon there are more stony ramparts ahead, those of Ramshaw Rocks, which border the highway closely and assume grotesque and individual appearances. These rocks are not small or single outcrops, but huge, humpy tors. To pass them on a moonlit night gives a lead to stories of prehistoric monsters, with spiky backs and wagging necks. A little ahead comes the final insight into the ancient world, the single isolated block of fantastic rocks called Hen Cloud. This formation, which might well be a part of the Dolomites, is one of the last playful flings of the gritstone which is the very backbone of the Pennines. Here at the end of the Pennine spine comes the comedy-drama which one scarcely expects from the stately, orderly range.

Nestling below Hen Cloud is the pleasant hamlet of **Upper Hulme**, situated on the River Churnet, here a meandering upland stream. The road climbs briefly, drops again for a mile, rises anew, and then through a cutting overlooks Leek, which is entered by a descending avenue. Leek is described on page 62. From Buxton to Leek directly is 12 miles.

The main route goes right along a lane at Flash Bar, and in a few hundred yards is encompassed closely by the stones of the mountain village of **Flash** (41). At 1,500 ft., Flash is one of the highest villages in the country. The experienced will recognize all the characteristics of an elevated settlement: the huddling together, the shelter of a hill to the north, the springs, the narrow and only street. Here, close to where Staffordshire, Derbyshire and Cheshire meet, lived the "flash men," coiners who gave a new expression to the English language.

From Flash a tolerable lane dips sharply by Flash Bottom to the River Dane above one of its choicest reaches at Gradbach (see page 36), and rejoins the main route above the few houses of Burntcliff Top. This is the way to go in bad weather or in the late evening instead of the following one.

From Flash village the thorough tourist should retrace his outward route to Flash Bar, going round the right-angled bend mentioned on page 34. At the next fork, however, only a few yards west, the way is leftward along a narrow lane which climbs over a low ridge. This ridge is the watershed, for while the nearby Dove goes southwards to the Trent and into the Humber and the North Sea, the stream in the next hollow is a tributary of the Dane, which finds its way to the Weaver and the Mersey and the Irish Sea.

There is a steep drop into the wild valley of this tributary. First the lane begins to climb rightwards, and then follows a precipitous drop to **Three Shire Heads**. Here the three counties of Staffordshire, Cheshire and Derbyshire meet at a tiny gritstone bridge. The scenery is all on a small scale: two tinkling brown brooks tippling out of mountain fastnesses, a few small trees crowding round the side of the watercourses, untamed slopes, bracken-covered, and, above all, hills shouldering out the sky. A remote and fanciful spot, yet only 30 miles from Manchester.

Beyond the bridge the route continues as a field road, which keeps high on the west bank of the River Dane past the farm of Cut-thorn, where the way is leftward along a gated road, through pastures bordering the stream. The final gate gives access near Burntcliff Top to a better road. A little ahead a minor highway drops leftward to Gradbach Mill, where the River Dane enters its most dramatic and least accessible reach.

From Gradbach Mill a path ascends through woods and by Castle Cliff Rocks (a fine view) to Ludschurch. A longer and more impressive approach, however, is from Danebridge (see page 38). From Burntcliff Top the high road, well above the north bank of the River Dane, follows the contour of a steep hillside through the yards of substantial gritstone farmhouses. Meanwhile the river, far below, flows through a deepening gorge. This stretch of highway is one of the most fascinating in the whole of Peakland—it is in Cheshire, of course—and the whole atmosphere seems charged with romance.

The by-road down the Dane Valley meets the Buxton-Congleton road at Allgreave, where there is an inn and a church. Hereabouts, or a little to the south-east at **Wincle** or at **Danebridge**, the non-hosteller ought to seek overnight accommodation. There is a little to be found, and if the worst comes to the worst, Macclesfield lies only 7 miles to the north-west through Clulow Cross and Sutton.

The hosteller should turn rightward at Allgreave, on the west side of the bridge, and follow the Clough Brook for a long half-mile to a fork. Here the valley road goes right up Wildboarclough (see page 37), but the way for Oakenclough Hostel leads leftward by Lower Nabbs Farm, later crossing a minor valley towards its head. Just short of a Saxon Cross (shown on Bartholomew's maps) a private road turns rightward to the hostel (49).

Oakenclough Hostel is situated amidst some of the finest of East Cheshire scenery, and makes a splendid weekending centre for Manchester, Potteries and Sheffield cyclists. The hostel is recommended to the tourist for a stay of two nights. Week-enders can readily adapt the day tour which follows to their own needs.

The hostel is built from local stone, and is a comparatively modern house amidst the moorland. Behind it, to the east, rises the characteristically Pennine dome of Shutlings Low (1,659 ft.), not the highest hill in the neighbourhood, but the most finely shaped.

———

The district is not one which should be hurried over. Its attractions are of the kind that need seeking out. Hence big mileages should not be tried. From the Saxon Cross go right by Hadden, where right again until a further fork above Langley Reservoirs. Here right again along a pleasant upland valley to a road junction at 1,179 ft. A short, sharp dip straight ahead (easterly) leads into **Wildboarclough**. This is probably the grandest of the valleys on the eastern edge of Peakland which are followed by a road. By going right, down-dale, the tourist soon senses that here is a memorable journey.

At first the Clough Brook is small and tinkling, and its dale is a mere channel through the moors which press down smoothly on both sides. The tourist will be reminded of the higher parts of the dales in the Scottish Borders and Northumberland. Below Clough House there are woodlands and a mill and cottages which do not mar the pleasure.

Beyond a church the dale becomes wider in its well, so that the brown stream wanders through meadows which contrast with the steepening valley sides and their crests of dark plantations. At the fork near Lower Nabbs Farm the previous day's route is regained. Immediately after the fork, going southward, there is a steep dip through an avenue and over a bridge. On quiet days the wheelman will find here a switchback sensation all ready made. The steep dip and the bridge provide a rare shoot—beyond the crown of the arch the bicycle seems to take off the ground.

At the Buxton-Congleton road the way is ahead along a minor road into Wincle, where a left turn just beyond the church leads to the fall into **Danebridge** (57). Here there are places where the bicycle can be left, while the excursion to Ludschurch is made afoot (see also page 36). From the east (or Staffordshire) side of the bridge a footpath first follows the stream northward, but in a few yards begins to climb rightward through woods, emerging in due course near Hangingstone Farm, where the way is to bear rightward below the crest of a ridge to the north. Soon Back Forest is entered, and then a track goes north-eastward to Ludschurch.

Lud's Church is a narrow passage between perpendicular rocks. It runs for about 200 yds. and is about two or three yards wide and of varying depths. Stunted ash, hazel and oak grow in the clefts, and a ship's figurehead adds to the bizarreness of the scene. The passage afoot through the crack is quite feasible. At the head, the open moor can be regained by way of a crude staircase. Near the head of the hollow is a deep cavity, into which the adventurous might squirm for some way.

The way back to Danebridge is by the outward route. About 2½ hrs. should be earmarked for the journey to and from Ludschurch.

A little north-west of the west side of Danebridge, near a few farm cottages, a gate will be seen. By going through this one of the most interesting little excursions in the district can be started—the trip alongside "The Feeder" to the Leek-Macclesfield road north of Rushton. This route—along which bicycles can be ridden for most of the way—begins as a field path which draws closer to the River Dane after the first few hundred yards. Then the river is crossed close to the entrance to "The Feeder," a conduit which serves the artificial Rudyard Lake with water. Alongside the waterway runs a path, narrow but quite practicable for cycling. The watershed hereabouts is so low that some of the water in the River Dane (which flows into the Weaver, as previously mentioned, and then into the Irish Sea) is transferred by way of "The Feeder" into the Lake, and from there by overflow into the Churnet and the North Sea.

The views of the **Dane Valley** as seen from the path are amongst the prettiest in the district. There are plenty of trees and pastoral meadows and many glimpses into a countryside which is not spoilt by too much motor traffic. "The Feeder" can be forsaken, within sight of the Leek-Macclesfield road, at a private drive. By going right, downhill, the main highway can be joined very easily about eight miles from Macclesfield (Macclesfield-Manchester, 18).

From this point it is a pleasant run southward to Rudyard Lake and the youth hostel on its west side. To reach the hostel the main road should be followed through Rushton village (its church stands in an isolated position on a hill to the west side of the road) and up a long hill curving up a slope by Rushton Marsh. Beyond the crossroads of Rycroft Gate a gate road on the right leads across the head of **Rudyard Lake** and round to the west (the quieter) side of the water to Cliffe Park Hall, the Rudyard Lake youth hostel. The building is a stout one; it has an excellent site overlooking the lake, and is a good winter week-ending haunt.

Rudyard Lake, although man-made, is a 2-mile stretch of narrow water. At its south end, which is popular with day trippers in summer, there are boats on hire. A pleasant woodland highway leads from the hostel to the south end. From this point it is about three miles to Leek (Leek to Newcastle-under-Lyme, 12 miles).

———————

From Rudyard Lake it is only about three miles of easy walking to the summit of Bosley Cloud. This tree-fringed height has a splendid prospect westward and northward across the Cheshire Plain.

The walk to Ludschurch will whet the appetite of the tourist for more of the romantic scenery of the Cheshire-Staffordshire border. From the east side of Danebridge a lane runs southward. Its course lies amongst dark plantations close to Swythamley Hall. At a fork the way is leftward into hillier country, going towards the coxcomb of The Roaches (see page 34). The highest point on this section of the route is gained at 1,322 ft. after a long walk. This is at the remote road junction of Clough Head. The way here is rightward, along the west side of The Roaches, which rise to the left in a knobbly fringe at the head of a stone-strewn wilderness. For 3 miles this road descends gradually to the south, dropping below Hen Cloud (see also page 35) to Upper Hulme and the Leek-Buxton road. Here the route goes leftward, climbing sharply to the north-west towards, the primeval contortions of Ramshaw Rocks (page 34). A mile from Upper Hulme, a moorland lane goes leftward, passing to the rear of Ramshaw Rocks and making for the isolated neighbourhood of Hazel Barrow. Here the way is right for a short way and then left across Goldstitch Moss. This is all bleak, but stirring, upland, dark and brooding. The previous day's route is reached near Gradbach Mill, whence the route described on page 36 should be taken back to Oakenclough youth hostel (73 miles). This round of 24 miles is one of the most attractive and remote in the Peak District.

Fresh pastures and more upland adventures lie ahead for the next day. From Oakenclough the route by Hadden to the head of Wildboarclough should be taken again. Then at Platting the dwindling dale should be forsaken for a lane going northward. Just short of the Buxton-Macclesfield road this forks. The way is right, and soon the main road is crossed. Next the lane begins to drop into the Ballgreave valley. On the right are great, swelling hills, aloof and untenanted. A climb follows to a fork, where the way is rightward (to the left lies Macclesfield) and steeply down, as in a Dartmoor lane, to the headwaters of the valley of the Todd Brook, which goes northward in a straight line. Soon, in a hollow to the right of the road, lies the ancient homestead of Saltersford Hall. Next comes a hairpin bend to the right at the small and secluded Jenkin Chapel. The next part of the road goes eastward and ascends sharply for a mile in a hollowed course—the certain sign of an old pack-horse road.

At the hill-top a road goes leftward along the summit of the ridge between the Todd Brook and the River Goyt—a fine panoramic route. About 1¼ miles along this road, and to the left, is **Windgather** Youth Hostel. The hostel is 1,200 ft. above sea level and in fine walking country. The hostel is on spartan lines. Close at hands are Windgather Rocks.

In the Todd Brook valley lies the village of Kettleshulme, picturesquely lining the Whaley Bridge-Macclesfield road as it drops to the bridge. (Manchester is 22 miles from Windgather by way of Kettleshulme, Whaley Bridge, Disley, High Lane, Hazel Grove and Stockport.

The through route goes straight on at the hilltop junction, gradually curving rightward and following the line of **The Street**, a Roman pathway. The going is both steep and rough, but the unfolding view is one of great beauty. The River Goyt has carved itself a glenlike course from the hills around the Cat and Fiddle, and man has aided nature by planting trees. Less of an attraction in this Highland setting is the Fernilee Reservoir, of the Stockport Corporation.

The road shortly reaches Goyts Bridge, about a mile above the head of the reservoir. Here, amidst picturesque surroundings in the pit of the vale, the wayfarer has a choice of two routes to Buxton.

To the east climbs the direct lane route to the Buxton-Manchester road. For nearly a mile the gradient is severe, but after crossing the line of the old High Peak railway there is a lessening of the steepness. This route gains the top of Long Hill, between Whaley Bridge and Buxton, about 1¼ miles north-west of the latter place, making 3½ miles from Goyts Bridge into Buxton.

The preferable way from Goyts Bridge to Buxton follows the sombre but romantic course of the upper Goyt—the county boundary between Cheshire and Derbyshire—along a fair road keeping to the west side of the stream and giving grand glimpses at its brown flood and rocky bed. This route emerges on the old road between Buxton and Macclesfield near Moss House (see page 33). A right turn and then a left give access to the modern Buxton-Macclesfield highway about 3½ miles out of Buxton. Into that resort it is mostly a pleasant drift downhill, from 1,500 ft. to 1,000 ft.

Buxton (90 miles), a bright and fresh town with accommodation to serve most tastes is described more fully on page 40. It forms a handy lunch halt. There is a youth hostel at Sherbrook Lodge, a mile south of Buxton on the Ashbourne road. Both bed-and-breakfast tourists and hostellers will probably prefer to seek the quieter neighbourhood of Millers Dale (see page 43).

From Buxton there follows one of the most impressive stretches of main road in the Peak. This is the valley of the Derbyshire Wye along the Bakewell road.

After nearly three miles of downhill going the highway is seen to rear ahead as it curls round the noble head of **Topley Pike**. Quarrying hereabouts, as elsewhere in the limestone district, is gradually ruining the picturesqueness of the scene.

From the foot of Topley Pike a by-road runs leftward with river and railway to the foot of Great Rocks Dale and the entrance to Chee Dale. (See page 71.)

To the right hereabouts lies Deepdale, one of the gems of the Peak District. It can be explored easily on foot—there is no road—after hiding the bicycle near its mouth. Deepdale is like a small Highland pass, without wood or water, and most impressive. There are several fissures in the dale, the most important being **Deepdale Cavern**. This is about a mile up the valley and on the left, or east side. The cave is about 100 yds. long, very dirty and requires careful negotiation.

On foot, a round starting at Buxton, might go by Cavedale, and up the slopes to the east and on to the bare moorland. About 1½ miles south-east of the cave stands the village of **Chelmorton**, close to Chelmorton Low. The village is 1,218 ft. above sea level, and therefore one of the highest in England.

The main route climbs sharply for 1½ miles round the northern face of Topley Pike, and close to the road summit reaches a fork road going leftward.

The Bakewell road continues straight ahead, shortly dropping through the slanted village of Taddington, and then descending into the well-wooded depths of Taddington Vale. At the eighth milestone from Buxton, and where the road flattens, **Monsal Dale** (see also page 44), through which flows the Wye, comes in from the left through a secluded, finely timbered valley. There is more of the pleasant valley going as the highroad paces down into the charming main-road village of **Ashford-in-the-Water**, now largely by-passed, and a place of many bridges and venerable old stone houses. The entry into Bakewell (11½ miles from Buxton) is a graceful one. Further details about Bakewell are on page 58.

From this fork there is a drop of 1½ miles through typical limestone country—stone walls running apparently at random, crowns of dark trees on isolated summits, waterless dales—into **Miller's Dale** (96½ miles), where the Wye comes in from the left after traversing Chee Dale (see pages 71–72).

Miller's Dale has a railway junction, but is situated on a splendid stretch of the River Wye. There is some overnight accommodation at Miller's Dale and more at **Tideswell** (see below) about three miles northward. The Miller's Dale youth hostel, at Ravenstor, some distance east of the station, stands high on a promontory at the junction of Miller's Dale and Tideswell Dale. The hostel is recommended for two nights' stay.

While the Miller's Dale district is particularly good as a walking centre—and those with plenty of time are advised to leave their bicycles at their headquarters and follow the route along the valley of the Wye, as described in reverse on page 71—the cyclist can see a great many of its attractions in a day's short but hard round.

In its course between Buxton and Bakewell the valley of the Wye has several names. Perhaps the finest reach is along Chee Dale (west of Miller's Dale—see page 71). Miller's Dale is next on its easterly path; while afterwards comes Cressbrook Dale, and then Monsal Dale. Unfortunately, between Miller's Dale and Cressbrook Dale there are factories, and the path linking the two reaches of the Wye is private. Walkers can use the path on payment of a toll, and it is possible for bicycles to be taken as well.

However, tourists who wish to ride through Monsal Dale, starting from Miller's Dale, can do so without keeping to stream level. This course involves a steady climb and a sharp drop, but introduces him to the upland village of Tideswell.

Miller's Dale is forsaken by a minor road which climbs between the grey crags of Tideswell Dale and in a long two miles reaches **Tideswell** (98½).

This is a large village of grey houses filling a hollow. Its principal attraction is the church, a beautiful structure commonly called "The Cathedral of the Peak."

A little east of the church a minor lane runs south-east over upland, and in a mile comes to Litton, where a right turn should be taken. This lane leads first over limestone upland and then sharply descends **Litton Slack**, once a noted test climb for motorists. Soon after the drop starts there is a spectacular peep to the right into the narrow gorge of the Wye.

The narrow, steepening lane invites care, and the tourist should be particularly alert for a sharp hairpin in the descent. When the valley is gained, the surroundings are sylvan. Feathery woodlands climb the vertical walk of the valley. Then the Wye comes alongside and is a silvery companion to the road as it threads Monsal Dale.

The main outlet from this part of Monsal Dale strikes steeply ahead and comes out of the valley on to open country at **Longstone Edge.** It is worth climbing the 500 yds. or so to this viewpoint, one of the most commanding in all Derbyshire.

Back in the dale, after descending the hill, a bridge crosses the Wye near the Monsal Dale railway station. This should be used to gain the west bank of the stream, and, at the cost of a little rough stuff, one of the most secluded stretches of riverside in the Peak. The path follows the Wye closely round a great curve in the dale. There are green riverside meadows and mountain trees and shapely hillside curves. On the opposite bank rises the graceful cone of Fin Cop. In this part of Monsal Dale the River Wye is at last free of the commercial taint which spoils so much of its earlier course. It is all Arcadian, a Derbyshire dale at its best.

The path emerges on the Buxton-Bakewell road about eight miles from the former place. Much of the path— it is about 1¾ miles long—can be ridden.

By going right the charming main-road scenery of Taddington Dale can be traversed en route for Miller's Dale. (This part of the route is described in full in reverse on page 43.) For 2 miles the road ascends until, just short of **Taddington**, it forks. A by-pass goes rightward while the old road (preferable) passes through the attractive village of Taddington, with its inns and catering houses. Two more miles of climbing leads to the Waterloo Inn and the summit of the long ascent. Short of the inn, a by-road turns rightward for Miller's Dale. The tourist can either take this or continue towards Buxton for a few hundred yards and take the main-road turn previously used into **Miller's Dale**, second time (110½). This round, although short, deserves to be travelled slowly and appreciatively. It repays every moment spent on it.

The next section of the tour traverses the limestone upland to Castleton, and goes on into the gritstone district at the south side of Kinder Scout. Up here, as around Arbor Low, the rolling hill country is full of interest.

The first 2 miles to Tideswell are identical with the route given for the previous day. The main route through the village should be followed, however, past the church and out to the Stony-Middleton-Chapel-en-le-Frith road at Lanehead. Here a by-road striking northward must be followed, past Little Hucklow. On the right can be seen the high ground severing this grey monotone of a landscape from the rich lands around the River Derwent to the east. Over at Great Hucklow, a mile or two east, modern drama and gliding have been encouraged in a village atmosphere.

From Little Hucklow or one of the lanes going right farther ahead the village of **Bradwell** can be entered. Almost the sole attraction of this scattered upland place is the **Bagshaw Cavern**, to the southwest of the village.

Resuming the main route, which follows the contours of a gentle slope whose crests lie a mile or so west, there is shortly a dip down Pin Dale, from which a wide view across the Vale of Hope is revealed to the striking undulations of the ridge running from Mam Tor in the west to Lose Hill in the east. The final entry into **Castleton** (120) lies down the steep zig-zags of Siggate, with its houses crowding towards the foot of the slope. Castleton and its caves are described fully on pages 59–61. It should be said, however, that for many years the townlet below Peveril Castle has been a weekend resort of Sheffield and Manchester cyclists. There is a large youth hostel at Castleton for those who wish to stay overnight, while there is also a selection of other accommodation. Those following this tour faithfully will find it a useful place for an early lunch. A full afternoon could then be devoted to seeing "the sights" before continuing to the recommended halt for overnight, Edale.

From Castleton it is an easy fall of 1½ miles into Hope, where a large church obstructs the main dale road and where the suburban influence of Sheffield (15 miles away) makes itself felt.

A mile beyond Hope, where the Bradwell Brook joins the River Noe (from Edale), there is the site of a Roman station close to the confluence.

A left turn in Hope leads into the Edale Valley, whose stream is the River Noe. The road first goes between the sentinel peaks of Lose and Win Hills, one on either hand, and soon gives a view straight ahead of the furrowed and frowning edges of Kinder Scout. First on the right and then on the left is the Dore and Chinley Railway, now part of the London Midland Region. The scene here is quite different from those on the limestone. Hereabouts the millstone grit predominates, with all its warmth and picturesqueness. The valley has a continuous and graceful curve, and from its well rise even slopes, culminating around bold hill buttresses on the north side in the impressive crests of Kinder's "edges."

Edale village (127½) lies up a subsidiary valley running northward out of the main dale. Down this comes tumbling the Grinds Brook, out of the Kinder massif, 1,200 ft. higher. There is hotel and other accommodation at Edale, which is recommended for at least two nights' stay. The youth hostel lies some three miles east, at Rowland Cote Farm, just north of the valley road between Hope and Edale. The mileage is given to Edale village, however, as a more recognizable point. The Rowland Cote Youth Hostel is a large, comfortable house.

A stay of two or three nights at Edale is advised.

One day might be spent profitably in making the ascent of Kinder Scout, a long, hard trip best undertaken in a small party. Full advice and directions may be had at the hostel. The ascent of Kinder Scout should not be attempted on a rainy or misty day. The grouse-shooting season, starting on August 12, also places limitations on visits.

Much less of a bog-trot and far more inviting because of its views is the ridge walk between Mam Tor and Lose Hill, a journey of some seven miles only, from either the hostel or Edale. This walk can be done as readily from Castleton, but then the distance is 9 miles.

From the Edale village lane-end, on the main valley road, there is a direct ascent to the south by footpath. It is easier, however, to go along the road up-dale as far as the hamlet of Barber Booth, there turning left across the River Noe and along the lane running southward and southeastward to **Mam Nick**. The prospect of the valley gradually unfolds during the ascent, the cloughs and edges of Kinder Scout on the opposite side being particularly impressive. The "nick" is a short, narrow pass, and from its summit the south side drops quickly to the Chapel-en-le-Frith-Castleton road. The walker will, however, leave the pass and climb towards the east. About 500 yds. of going leads to the summit of **Mam Tor**, or the "Shivering Mountain," 1,700 ft. above sea level. The hill commands a full view of the Hope Valley, with Castleton laid out as on a chart to the south. The name "Shivering Mountain" arises from the steep south-east face being composed of alternate layers of gritstone and shale. The surface of this face slips under pressure from extreme weather.

The ridge walk from Mam Tor to Lose Hill (pronounced *Loose* Hill) is the finest of its kind in Peakland. It really is a ridge, almost a razor-edge in places. The finest individual feature of the ridge walk is Back Tor, shortly before Lose Hill. Back Tor is an almost perpendicular face of gritstone arising from a piece of woodland in which hazel and birch predominate. Lose Hill (1,563 ft.) looks across the narrow mouth of Edale at the opposite height of Win Hill

(1,523 ft.). The descent into the valley continues in a south-easterly direction along the shoulder of the hill. The valley road is joined near a bridge across the Noe, about a mile north of Hope. Castleton sojourners turn right for Hope and Castleton, while those for Rowland Cote and Edale go left. There is some public transport along both routes.

A short walk from Edale village leads up the Grinds Brook Clough, a deeply cut watercourse between gritstone overlain by peat.

A day's run from and to Edale or Rowland Cote will take in the northern part of Peakland and introduce the tourist to the Snake Road and the Derwent Dams. From Edale the road by Barber Booth to Mam Nick should be taken first. This involves a stiff climb—mostly walkable—early in the day. The Castleton-Chapel-en-le-Frith road (130) is gained about 2½ miles above the former place. A right turn (caution) leads along the main road for another 1½ miles of climbing, with the long shoulder of Rushup Edge on the right, after which comes a steady fall of 2 miles to near **Chapel-en-le-Frith** (135), which is entered by a short rise. The town is an old one, now partly industrialized. At the top of the rise, on the right, there is a small market place which has an old cross and stocks.

A right turn, for "Hayfield," should be taken in "Chapel." This soon descends, and then rises again amongst the legs of tall, striding railway viaducts. At the next fork the way is rightward.

To the left goes a side-road which runs with the railway through Buxworth (formerly Bugsworth—the inhabitants changed the name within recent memory), and so to the Buxton-Manchester road, about 16 miles from the latter place.

An alternative route to Manchester—the main one—goes straight ahead in Chapel-en-le-Frith, and continues down a pleasant valley to Whaley Bridge (Chapel-en-le-Frith to Manchester, direct 20½ miles).

A steady climb of 1½ miles leads to Chinley Head. On the left, a pastoral valley can be seen. Just left of the summit there is a farm,

pleasingly and aptly named "Peep-o'-Day." A fall of 1½ miles brings
the traveller amongst the dwellings of **Hayfield** (139), a mill town
on the edge of the moorlands and a gateway to the Kinder Scout
district. There are teahouses and inns at Hayfield for lunch halts.

The ascent out of Hayfield, on the road northward, is reminiscent
of the earlier climb out of Chapel en-le-Frith. In about a mile,
however, there are pleasant parklands, although just beyond rise the
primeval, untilled bogs which stretch over Kinder Scout. Two miles
up from Hayfield comes the Grouse Inn.

Just before the inn, a lane goes leftward across the open
moorland, passing on the left in a few yards the "Abbot's Chair,"
probably the socket of a boundary cross. The lane soon afterwards
begins to drop down the Monk's Road, and enters the village of
Charlesworth, crossing (caution) the Stockport-Glossop road. The
fall continues into Broadbottom, where there is another impressive
railway viaduct, and then begins a climb into the village of
Mottram-in-Longden-dale, which has an imposing hill-top
church to the right.

At a crossroads in the village, a left turn may be taken for Hyde
and Manchester, or the road ahead may be used for Stalybridge,
Ashton-under-Lyne, Oldham and Rochdale, passing first through
Mottram Cutting.

This route is a useful—if hilly and rough—alternative to the main
roads between the Peak and the South Lancashire and North
Cheshire towns at weekends or other times of congestion.

After the Grouse Inn there is a drop of 2 miles through Chunal
into **Glossop** (143½), of which there is further mention on page 62.
The town is entered by Charlestown Road and Victoria Street.

Hard riders could profitably extend their journey by a more
northerly loop than the main journey described later. This is by
Woodhead, the Flouch Inn, Ewden Beck and the Strines Inn to
Bamford, Hope and Edale again (see also page 19).

From Glossop the Snake Road is reached by going eastward

along High Street East and Sheffield Road. Beyond a bridge the road begins to climb in earnest, and soon the suburbs are left behind. For 4½ miles the climb persists without any great slackening. The highway was built for coaching in 1821, and considering the obstacles is very well engineered. The average gradient is about 1 in 15, and the climb can be ridden throughout by a tourist who uses low gears. In reverse the descent is a splendid one. **The Snake** is not a pass, although often erroneously called one. Anything less like a narrow pass than the exposed summit of the road could hardly be imagined.

The first feature of the ascent is the round, wooded shape of Shire Hill, on the left at the head of a long initial drag. At the foot of this mound the highway sheers off to the right, and for 500 yds. mounts a hillside. Where the road bends leftward it is worth getting off the bicycle, crossing the road cautiously and looking down at the reservoir, filling the valley of the Hurst Brook below. To the left lies a steadily-rising slope of typical Pennine desolation: peat broken by masses of stones. At the 21st milestone from Sheffield, road and brook have drawn together and they go forward to the exposed flats of the summit, 1,680 ft.

Ahead the moors seem to swallow the road as it dips into the first clough on the south-east side. In less than a mile, however, the layout can be comprehended. Instead of being laid mostly across open moor, as on the Glossop side, the road is cunningly contrived along the side of a bare upland dale.

Down the first side-valley on the left comes the path from **Doctor's Gate** (see page 70). Soon the slope climbing leftward steepens greatly, and a few more hardy trees begin to appear. The first deep opening on the right, seen just before the 17th milestone from Sheffield, is **Ashop Clough** (see pages 69–70), which carries a path over the north-west shoulder of Kinder Scout to Hayfield (page 49). Almost immediately afterwards comes the first inhabited building for 6 miles, the **Snake Inn**, snugly situated to the left of the road.

All this is fine downhill going, which is doubly exciting when the wind comes from the west. After the inn the gradients are not as steep. Instead there are plantations and softer valley scenery to charm. A reminder of the closeness of the savage tops, however, can be seen in the bulging buttress of Fairbrook Naze, to the right, a thousand feet higher than the road and thrusting forward between the Ashop and Fair Brooks. Just before the 15th milestone from Sheffield it is worth hiding the bicycle for an hour or so and exploring the lovely valley of the Alport Clough.

After Alport Bridge the run downward becomes more beautiful still, as the woodlands thicken. There are plenty of river peeps for a mile or two, and then the road reaches the north side of the great **Ladybower Reservoir** of the Derwent Valley Water Board.

The road now crosses the main valley (which runs northwards) by an embankment and a bridge which makes a good viewpoint. It is difficult to remember that only a few years ago all the water-filled hollows to the west, north, east and south were graceful valleys and that close to where they met stood the fine square form of the Ashopton Inn.

A mile or two up Derwent-dale was Derwent Hall Youth Hostel, a gracious building close by a venerable pack-horse bridge. The embankment of the new Ladybower Reservoir is the largest in England. It was completed early in the 1939-45 war.

———————

Just before the bridge over the northern tongue of the Ladybower Reservoir a new road goes leftward along the west side of the water. This is now the road to the two older dams (built in 1900-12) which hold back reservoirs higher up the dale. Formerly a road ran up the east side, past Derwent Hall. The new road reaches the foot of the Derwent Reservoir, at Fairholmes, where the tourist can cross to the east side of the water or keep to the west. The two old reservoirs are great sheets of water amid wild moorland slopes, which have been tamed in appearance by plantations. The east-side road is the shortest way to the head of the lakes, but the west side, especially where it twines into the heart of the clough formed by the River Westend, on the highest reservoir—the Howden—is the more picturesque, although longer. It is possible to do a round of the reservoirs, going up one side and down the other along gated roads to which bicycles are admitted. At the head of the Howden Reservoir is Slippery Stones, where the path of Cut Gate (see pages 70–71) commences. It is recommended that the road along the west side be taken to

Slippery Stones, returning by the east side. This makes a total of about 16 miles from and to the Snake Road at the new bridge.

Across the bridge, on the east side, the road rises to the **Ladybower Inn** (157½). Here the way is rightward, down Derwent-dale, and through Bamford to Bamford Station, through a wide valley along a good road commanding a view of Win Hill to the west. At Bamford Station the route goes rightward into the Noe Valley and Hope, where rightwards again for Rowland Cote and Edale (162), making a total round of 34½ miles, in its simplest form.

Leaving Edale or Rowland Cote finally, the road down the dale must be traced again to Hope, and then the Hope and Derwent Valleys followed through a countryside which is pleasant enough but with little calling for comment.

At **Hathersage** (172) there is plenty to see, however, and as a centre for walks amongst the millstone-grit region to the north and east it has no rival. Northward runs the beautiful course of the Hood Brook, and above this rises the long, bold front of Stanage Edge, a typical Pennine crest of rocks and boulder. Closer to the village, on the east side, and within a two-hour return walk, stands Higgar Tor, which has great blocks of gritstone on its summit. A little south is the oblong-shaped fortification called Cark Wark, believed to be a prehistoric stronghold.

Hathersage is chiefly renowned, however, for the reputed grave of Little John, who was also said to have been born in the village. The grave is in the churchyard, south of the graceful church, and is marked by two small inscribed stones, 10 ft. apart.

The whole of this district is recommended for a thorough exploration, and the hosteller should make his way for nearly two miles down the delightful valley road on the west side of the River Derwent to the entrance to **Leam Hall** Youth Hostel (174). Although hostels are normally closed in the middle of the day, it is generally possible to find somewhere to leave heavy kit and to do the rest of the day's adventuring with cape, light refreshments and tools only. Non-hostellers might seek overnight accommodation in Hathersage or at attractively-situated **Grindleford Bridge,** a mile farther on than the hostel drive.

Leam Hall Youth Hostel, with accommodation for 80, stands high above the valley in its own grounds, and with a fine prospect over the Derwent at Millstone Edge and the woods of the Longshaw Estate. Inside the latter is the Longshaw Guesthouse, of the Holiday Fellowship. The house is situated in National Trust property, and is a fine centre for a long stay by the walker or cyclist.

After leaving touring kit behind, the road should be regained and the outward road taken to a point just short of the Derwent Bridge, south of Hathersage. Here a lane goes leftward, climbing steeply through woods to a terrace above the Highlow Brook, which later becomes **Abney Clough.** This is a particularly fine example of a romantic Pennine dale, short, steep and half-hidden. The narrow road along its northern edge gives grand panoramic views of the hollow. The head of the dale is crossed beyond a tiny church in the neat and remote hamlet of Abney, and thereafter traverses open moorland by Abney Grange and rounds Hucklow Edge, leaving the village of Great Hucklow to the south.

Next the route runs eastward along the direct Sir William Road, the old thoroughfare between Tideswell and Peak Forest to Sheffield, and said to be named after Sir William Peveril. The first, and only, village along this is **Bretton.** Here there is a small cottage youth hostel (on the road leading down into Bretton Clough to the north), which will be preferred by some to Leam Hall. The bicycle might be left at or near the hostel and the walk down into the clough taken, a distance of about two miles return. The clough is even more striking than Abney Clough to the north. It is so remote that the Britons are reputed to have driven their herds into it to keep them from the Romans.

At an altitude of 1,324 ft., about three-quarters of a mile beyond Bretton, a road goes rightward for Eyam. This is the way to take. (Sir William Road continues straight ahead and drops into Grindleford Bridge, about two miles east.)

Through Highcliffe this lane wanders along a slope running east above Eyam village, which can be seen nestling in a hollow to the south. Then comes another road junction. Here the way is rightward for Eyam. To the left, however, lies Mompesson's Well. The rightward turn leads steeply downhill into Eyam Village.

Eyam figures in the history books because of the heroism of its villagers when the plague reached it from London in the year 1665, in a bundle of tailor's samples. The plague raged throughout that autumn and broke out again in the following summer, 79 persons dying in August alone.

Eyam is a pretty village situated on a slope, and amongst its domestic dwellings there is plenty of character. The church, however, is the most interesting building. It dates from early in the 17th century, and has a pinnacled tower. Southwest of the church is the Cucklet Church, a limestone rock overlooking a grassy dell.

From Eyam, Grindleford Bridge and Leam Hall can be regained by a good road going east and then north round a projecting shoulder of hill. An alternative, slightly longer way, is to go for half a mile southward down the narrow, tree-shrouded road through Eyam Dale to Middleton Dale, rather wider and with a brook on its south side. The way at the road junction is leftward. (Middleton Dale lies on the upland route between Manchester and Chesterfield, [for Lincolnshire], via Chapel-en-le-Frith, Peak Forest, Stony Middleton, Baslow and Wadshelf.) Stony Middleton is a scattered and rather untidy village filling the mouth of Middleton Dale. Beyond it comes Calver Sough, where a left turn and then another lead pleasantly along the west side of the Derwent back into Grindleford Bridge, for **Leam Hall.** (Second time, 189 miles. Leam Hall or Grindleford, using above round, return 15 miles.)

A short evening or early morning round from Leam Hall or Grindleford Bridge which ought on no account to be missed takes in the Longshaw Estate, Froggatt Edge, the Toad Rock and "The Surprise View." This little excursion should be done in an anti-clockwise direction, otherwise much of its beauty is missed, especially "The Surprise." Moreover, during the mid-day hours, especially on a Sunday, it is inclined to be very busy with coaches and cars. As a before-breakfast spin from Grindleford Bridge it could scarcely be bettered.

From Grindleford Bridge the Sheffield highway must be followed towards the north-east. This first crosses the River Derwent at a lovely reach, and then ascends steadily through the suburbanized hamlet of Nether Padley. Soon the Dore and Totley railway line can be seen running up the valley after emerging from the tunnel under Totley Moor. Later on, the "edge" on the right draws closer and there is a fine belt of woodland between the crest and the road. Down below a minor stream runs down through a little wilderness of its own. The rise lasts for 2 miles, and then on the right the entrance to the Longshaw Estate can be seen. Those with plenty of time are advised to leave their bicycles at the lodge and wander afoot through the grounds.

The road, however, bends leftward—a right turn would lead to the nearby Fox House Inn, and the roads to Sheffield by Eccleshall and to Dronfield by Owler Bar (see page 88)—and across open, boulder-strewn moor drops to the rocky course of the Burbage Brook. Immediately beyond the bridge stands the Toad Rock, as close an imitation of the reptile as need be. A mile ahead, though, comes an even greater natural wonder, "**The Surprise**." The road has on its left a wild stretch of fairly level land, while on the right are high, jutting rocks and boulders. Going round one of these the eye is suddenly arrested by the view which appears ahead. Beyond a low retaining wall the Derwent Valley immediately opens out in a wide and varied prospect.

The remainder of the way down into Hathersage has less incident. It is a lively enough descent of 1½ miles, however. From Hathersage back to Leam Hall or Grindleford Bridge is already familiar to the tourist. (Leam Hall or Grindleford Bridge, third time, 8 miles.) (Total mileage of tour, 197.) Leam Hall is the nearest of all hostels to Sheffield for those making for the grandest parts of Peakland. The handiest way of reaching it from the two stations in Sheffield is by way of Eccleshall, Foxhouse and Grindleford Bridge, 12 miles.

On leaving Leam Hall or Grindleford Bridge, the easy road down to Calver Sough should be used. At the crossroads the leftward turn is the one to prefer. It leads across the Derwent and keeps close to the river to **Baslow**.

By going straight ahead in Calver Sough, a pretty main-road route can be followed to Hassop Station. Here a right turn leads by

Ashford, Taddington and Topley Pike to Buxton, while Bakewell may be gained by going straight ahead.

Baslow (202) is a busy crossroads village. For tourists it is most noteworthy as the nearest large centre to the grounds of **Chatsworth House**. These can be traversed by bicycle, and form a welcome change from orthodox roadfaring. From Baslow an avenue road running southward should be taken. The first important fork to the right leads to Bakewell, but the Chatsworth-bound should keep straight on over a hill reaching 573 ft., fork left again, and so into the grounds down a long, unfenced approach. Deer may be seen amongst the glades and in the parkland. Soon the "model" village of **Edensor** is reached on the right. All kinds of architecture can be seen in Edensor's frontages, and the ducal influence is marked. Across the River Derwent, on rising ground, can be observed the great mass of Chatsworth House, a seat of the Dukes of Devonshire. The public is generally admitted mid-week at a small fee.

Through the meadows and round the trees winds the public highway through the park. It leads eventually to a bridge across the Derwent and then past the village of Beeley to the main Buxton-Matlock road at Little Rowsley. Across the river and railway, in Great Rowsley, stands the old-fashioned Peacock Inn.

From Little Rowsley the main road should be followed by the railway noise and dirt of Rowsley and Darley Dale. The latter is a pleasant enough village, with many nurseries and market gardens, and has in its churchyard a venerable yew, said to vie with that at Fortingal, in Perthshire (see Cycling Guide No. 3, Scottish Highlands) in antiquity.

Darley Dale is broad, and therefore when the valley contracts to traverse Matlock Dale it is all the more surprising. River, road and railway are trammelled at Matlock between tall limestone cliffs already much quarried in parts.

Matlock (213) is described fully on pages 63–64. The riverside road remains full of interest past Cromford, where the first cotton mills in England were built, and by the point where the High Peak Railway commences its sensational traverse at High Peak Junction, and by Whatstandwell, with its view of the Crich Stand war memorial on the hilltop to the left. The Derwent is crossed here, and the east bank followed past Ambergate Junction and on with the widening valley through the industrial town of Belper to Milford and **Derby**, the starting point (230 miles).

Those who wish to see more of the Matlock district could break their journey for a further night, staying at Matlock or at the youth hostels at Wirksworth or at Shining Cliff, west of Ambergate. The latter is the nearest hostel to Derby, and very useful for those wishing to take a train home from that town, which is about 13 miles away.

The district west of Matlock, including the Via Gellia road and the Bonsall area, are described under "Matlock," on pages 63–64.

This round of 230 miles in 13 days could be curtailed into an eight-day tour or extended to cover 15 days, by staying longer at some of the halting-places. As given, the halts are at Ilam Hall or Ashbourne (three nights); Wildboarclough or Danebridge district (two nights); Miller's Dale, Buxton or Tideswell (two nights); Rowland Cote or Edale (three nights); and Leam Hall or Grindleford Bridge (two nights). The Peak District is so small that for detailed exploration more than one night should be spent at every halting-place. It is also worth remembering that with Manchester and Sheffield so close to the district, most of the youth hostels are heavily booked for Saturday nights throughout the year. Therefore advance booking is most desirable.

GAZETTEER

ASHBOURNE. M.D., Sat. E.C.D., Wed. (Birmingham, 42; Burton-upon-Trent, 19; Buxton, 20½; Derby, 13; Leek, 15; Leicester, 42; Lichfield, 26; Macclesfield, 28; Manchester, 45; Matlock, 13½; Newcastle-under-Lyme, 25; Nottingham, 28½; Sheffield, 35; Stafford, 26; Uttoxeter, 12; London, 139 miles.) A pleasant town, the closest of large places to the scenery of Dovedale and the Manifold Valley, and reached by good roads from the south, east and west. In its main street is a 16th-century grammar school and the Pegg Almshouses, dating from 1669. The church, to the west of the town centre, has a spire 212 ft. high and figures in all glimpses of Ashbourne. There is a variety of overnight and cafe accommodation in Ashbourne.

BAKEWELL. E.C.D., Thurs. (Ashbourne, 18; Birmingham, 60; Buxton, 12; Chesterfield, 13; Derby, 26; Leeds, 48½; Leek, 18½; Lichfield, 44; Manchester, 37; Matlock, 8; Nottingham, 33½; Sheffield, 16½; London, 152.)

Perhaps the pleasantest of all the Derbyshire townlets and a useful centre for the River Wye and its tributaries. A graceful bridge crosses the river, and south of it there is a well-planned public park on the river banks. The church, with an octagonal tower and spire, is backed by wooded hills, and in the churchyard there is a Saxon Cross. Inside there is much to see—the Vernon Chapel and effigies of the Vernon and Manners families being noteworthy.

BUXTON. M.D., Sat. E.C.D., Wed. (Ashbourne, 20½; Bakewell, 12; Birmingham, 62½; Chester, 48½; Chesterfield, 24½; Derby, 33; Glossop, 15; Huddersfield, 36; Leeds, 51; Leek, 12½; Lichfield, 46½; Liverpool, 52½; Macclesfield, 12; Manchester, 25; Matlock, 20; Nottingham, 45½; Sheffield, 28½; Shrewsbury, 56½; Stafford, 36; Warrington, 35; London, 159.) The largest town in "the interior" of Derbyshire, 1,000 ft. above sea level, and a fine centre for the valley scenery of the upper parts of the Rivers Wye, Goyt, Dane, Dove and Manifold and for the broad moorlands dividing them. Its springs were known to the Romans. The chief shopping street, called Spring Gardens, confines the London-Manchester road to a narrow channel. The Crescent, built in 1780-84, at a cost of £120,000, is a stately Palladian block. Dominating the west side of the town is the 154-ft. dome of the Devonshire Hospital (originally a ducal riding school). The dome is larger than those of St. Peter's, Rome, or St. Paul's Cathedral, London. Poole's Hole, south-west of the town along Temple Road, is a natural cavern about half a mile long.

There is a very wide choice of overnight accommodation in Buxton, including a youth hostel in its own grounds just south of the town, on the Ashbourne Road. Taddington, along the Bakewell road, is some 1,050 ft. above sea level and a claimant to the title of the highest village in England. Flash village, south of Buxton, and just west of the Leek road (see pages 34–35) is much higher, however, at 1,684 ft.

Of the principal roads from Buxton, that over the Cat and Fiddle to Macclesfield (see pages 33–34) is the highest, the one to Leek (pages 34–35) the most interesting, that to Ashbourne (pages 7-8) the dullest, the Bakewell road the prettiest (page 42), the Chapel-en-le-Frith highway the most industrialized, and the one by Long Hill to Whaley Bridge for Manchester the busiest.

CASTLETON. E.C.D., Wed. (Buxton, 11; Chapel-en-le-Frith, 8; Sheffield, 16.) The best centre for exploration of the limestone caverns of Peakland. Busy at weekends and with a youth hostel (in the centre of the village, at Castleton Hall) and other places providing overnight accommodation. Industrial developments to the east detract somewhat from its attractiveness.

The village itself stands mostly to the south of the main road from Buxton and Chapel-en-le-Frith to Hathersage and Sheffield. It has its old-fashioned corners and a church with a Norman doorway.

Peveril Castle, immediately south of the village, is the dominating feature of Castleton, and from it the village derives its name. The castle is perched on a bold spur of rock between Cave Dale and the entrance to Peak Cavern. It was built by William Peveril, son of William the Conqueror, as related in Scott's romance, "Peveril of the Peak." The remains consist of a square keep and part of a former encircling wall. Because of its almost impregnable position, the castle is hard to approach, but a zig-zag path leads up on the village side.

Amongst the pleasantest of short evening walks from Castleton is the one up Cave Dale. The entrance to this is from the Tideswell ("Siggate") road at the south-east corner of the square. The walk of half a mile up Cave Dale gives a fine impression of the crags and precipices of Peveril Castle.

Castleton is, however, most noted for its caverns. There are several of these, but an energetic visitor might see two of them, Peak Cavern and the Speedwell Mine, or the Blue John Mine or Treak Cliff Mine, in the course of a long afternoon. All are commercialized, and a charge is asked from all who want to see the bowels of the earth.

The nearest cave to the village is the Peak Cavern, and the tourist in a hurry could take a look up Cave Dale, climb to the castle and back and visit the Peak Cavern in the course of 2½ rather strenuous hours.

On the west side of the village a clear stream runs, and by following this towards its source, the huge, gaping mouth of Peak

Cavern can be seen very quickly. The water actually issues from a gushing spring, called the Russet Well, on the left, just before the entrance to the cave.

The imposing appearance of the mouth of the Peak Cavern consists of a high natural archway under the steep rock face, which is crowned by the castle. At the far end of the outer cave a small door gives access to a narrow passage leading into an inner chamber called the Bell House. There is a gloomy watercourse beyond and then further chambers, including one called Roger Rain's House, where the drippings from the roof can be quite drenching after heavy rain in the outer world. The final chamber is again bell-shaped.

The next underground attraction is the Speedwell Mine, about 1,400 yards from the village, and just south of the main Chapel-en-le-Frith road, along the former coaching highway to Buxton through the Winnats. There are some outbuildings that mark the entrance to the mine.

First of all there is a descent down about 100 rough-hewn steps. At the foot of this staircase a narrow canal is found cut through the rock. Along the canal visitors are propelled for about 800 yds. in boats. The canal is quite straight and ends at the Grand Cavern and the Bottomless Pit. From a platform the eyes, helped by artificial light, seek to find the roof of the cavern—it is about 500 ft. high. Water pours into the pit, and about 100 ft. below the platform flows away as a stream.

From so much subterranean wandering it is a change to visit an above-ground marvel. This is the **Winnats Pass**, which can be explored by continuing past the entrance to the Speedwell Mine. "The Winnats" (i.e., "The Wind Gates") as a limestone pass is comparable with the Cheddar Gorge (see Cycling Guide No. 4, "South-West England"), although the scale is far smaller. The Winnats Gorge is a steep climb flanked by slopes which are almost perpendicular. The old road—up which a bicycle may be pushed easily enough to the Buxton and Chapel-en-le-Frith highways, generally reached by the longer Mam Tor route—has a loose surface and winds steadily up the pass.

By continuing afoot up the busy main road towards Mam Tor— or after walking some way up the Winnats and returning—the next objective of the underworld explorer is the Blue John Mine. Once again the entrance might well pass unnoticed. A doorway in the hillside gives access to steps and then to a narrow but high corridor in which crystals are well exposed. A spacious chamber called Lord Mulgrave's Dining Room gives way to a further cave, which has a roof 250 ft. high. There are stalagmites and stalactites in this, and also the "Blue John" stone in places.

Also in the Mam Tor direction is the latest of the Castleton caves to be opened up to the public. This is the Treak Cliff Cavern, first made generally accessible in 1935.

The main road to Buxton and "Chapel" takes a sweeping turn to the left as it ascends the face of Mam Tor, which hill rises boldly, its "shivering" face exposed to the south-east. In a depression between the "Chapel" and Buxton roads, after they fork at the head of the Mam Tor road climb, and rather difficult to find, is Giant's Hole. It is a treacherous and uncommercialized cave, narrow and dirty, and entered by a shaft which is nearly vertical.

About 3½ miles along the Buxton road the prominent nose of Eldon Hill can be seen. On the south side of this and best approached by a lane commencing at the north-west end of the upland village of Peak Forest (on the "Chapel"-Stony Middleton road) lies Eldon Hole. This is gained by going, through Old Dam, there turning leftward and then rightward along a minor lane which heads towards the east side of Eldon Hill. Eldon Hole can be reached then across fields on the left. The hole is a vertical fissure in the limestone, and it was once considered fathomless.

Castleton keeps up one of its old customs. The whole village does honour to Old Apple Day, May 29, with merrymaking which begins with a procession of dancers and musicians in attendance on a chosen king and queen.

DERBY. M.D., Fri. E.C.D., Wed. (Ashbourne, 13; Bedford, 78; Birmingham, 39½; Buxton, 33; Chesterfield, 25½; Coventry, 40; Doncaster, 53½; Leeds, 70; Leicester, 28; Lincoln, 51½; Macclesfield, 41; Manchester, 58; Mansfield, 24; Matlock, 18; Northampton, 60; Nottingham, 15½; Sheffield, 37; Shrewsbury, 63; Stafford, 32; Stamford, 53; Stoke-on-Trent, 35; Warrington, 64; London, 126 miles.)

The southern gateway to the Peak District. The by-pass road to the south should be shunned by the cyclist, who would do well to remember that the direct routes through the town are shortest for him in distance and time. Derby shows little of its antiquity. It was a Roman station, was held for Parliament throughout the Civil War, and in 1745 represented the farthest penetration into England of the forces of Prince Charles Edward. The Highlanders actually reached Cavendish Bridge, to the south-east, on the London road.

The Perpendicular tower of All Saints is one of the sights of Derby. Nine miles south of Derby is Castle Donington, where stands Donington Park, famous before the 1939-45 war as a venue for bicycle, motorcycle and car racing.

GLOSSOP. E.C.D., Tues. (Barnsley, 24; Buxton, 15; Chesterfield, 33; Derby, 42; Huddersfield, 22; Leeds, 37; Macclesfield, 19; Manchester, 14; Matlock, 35; Oldham, 12; Sheffield, 24½; Stockport, 11; London, 174 miles.)

A rough-and-ready manufacturing town at the west side of the Snake Road, and a convenient point of entry into the Peak District from East Lancashire and West Yorkshire (see Cycling Guide No. 1). The town can be skirted on the west by riders making for Hayfield from the Mottram Cutting direction. North-east of the town stretches the wild region of Longdendale, a valley of reservoirs next to the unpathed fastnesses of Bleaklow (between Crowden and the Snake Road), the wildest piece of England south of the Cheviots.

LEEK. M.D., Wed. E.C.D., Thurs. (Ashbourne, 15; Buxton, 12½; Derby, 28; Macclesfield, 13; Manchester, 31; Newcastle-under-Lyme, 12; London, 154 miles.)

A textile and market town at the south-west corner of Peakland. It stands on a hill and has steep streets. Through it passes the important Macclesfield-Derby main road.

MACCLESFIELD. M.D., Sat. E.C.D., Wed. (Altrincham, 16; Ashbourne, 28; Buxton, 12; Chester, 36; Chesterfield, 36; Crewe, 23; Derby, 41; Glossop, 19; Leek, 12½; Manchester, 18; Sheffield, 36; Stockport, 11½; Stoke-on-Trent, 22½; Warrington, 23; London, 167 miles.)

A convenient point of approach to the Peak District from Liverpool and the railway junction of Crewe. Macclesfield is interested in silk and other textiles industrially, but topographically has a most attractive situation.

MATLOCK. M.D., Tues. and Fri. E.C.D., Thurs. (Ashbourne, 13½; Buxton, 20; Cheadle (Staffs), 26½; Chesterfield, 10½; Derby, 18; Glossop, 35; Leek, 23½; Lichfield, 40; Macclesfield, 32; Manchester, 45; Mansfield, 17½; Newark, 36; Newcastle-under-Lyme, 38; Nottingham, 26; Sheffield, 22; London, 144 miles.)

A ribbon-growth of a resort along the course of the Derwent. The site is naturally beautiful, and much of it remains so, but extensive quarrying of the limestone rock has spoilt much of the dale. Coming from the south, river and road enter the Matlock Gorge at Cromford.

Matlock Bath lies mostly on the green slopes to the west of the highway and the river. Opposite, the rocky slopes drop sharply to the riverside. Here, too, is the pump room, and outside it an artificial pond in which large, odd and rainbow-hued fish disport themselves. There are plenty of caverns to see at Matlock, most of them old mine workings, and all commercialized. Most of the caves lie on the west side of the river. Matlock Bath is shut in from the northwest by the Heights of Abraham, commanding a fine view. Farther away in the same direction is Masson, a hill rising to 1,110 ft.

The main road runs up Matlock Dale, which has too many reminders of industry to be wholly satisfying. On the east side of the river and reached by a bridge near Matlock Bath Station, is High Tor, perhaps the most distinctive natural feature about Matlock. The height is 380 ft. above the river, and dominates Matlock Dale. Matlock Bridge, the most northerly of the valley Matlocks, is the business district, and its station (called "Matlock") is the most important in the region, and a good starting-point for the south end of the Peak District. Many of the St. Pancras-Manchester (Central) trains stop at Matlock.

Matlock Bank, to the north-east of Matlock Bridge, lies on a slope, and its most prominent building is Smedley's Hydro. To the south and on the slopes to the east of the Derwent also are Matlock Green and Old Matlock, the latter the original village, with old houses. The garish building to the south-east is Riber Castle, a landmark erected by Smedley late in the last century.

South-west of the Matlocks lies a countryside which repays careful exploration. From Cromford a side road runs westward by mill pools in a valley to the foot of the Via Gellia. A right turn leads up a minor dale into Bonsall, a quaint village with a picturesque church, a cross on a pedestal and many springs. The Via Gellia has nothing to do with the Romans, but is so named after the Gells, a noted family in these parts.

HIGH TOR.

Cycling in the Peak District today

As Harold Briercliffe wrote this cycle route guide in 1949, many of the roads he mentions are now busier than they were and not suitable for cycling today. Suggested alternative cycle routes, from Sustrans, which are in the same location as Harold's original route are listed below. To devise your own route and map, go to www.sustrans.org.uk for online mapping, free iphone and android apps.

There are numerous wonderful traffic-free, family-friendly rides in the Peak District, which form part of the long-distance routes of the National Cycle Network that run through the region.

National Route 6 runs for approximately 68 miles between **Derby** and **Sheffield** in the Peak District area. The majority of this route is traffic-free, including a converted railway path from Blidworth to Sherwood Forest.

Perhaps the most recognised long-distance National Cycle Route in the Peak District is the **Pennine Cycle Way**, which in its entirety runs approximately 460 miles from **Derby** to **Berwick-Upon-Tweed** via **Hebden Bridge** and **Appleby.** One highlight of the Pennine Cycle Way in the Peak District is the **Tissington Trail** – a glorious 13-mile traffic-free converted railway path that links Ashbourne to Parsley Hay, passing through the picturesque village of Tissington. The trail also passes near to Dovedale, a dramatic limestone ravine with stunning scenery and wildlife that is famous for its much-loved stepping stones that cross the River Dove.

The Tissington Trail is one of an excellent trio of traffic-free cycle routes in the Peak District that all interconnect. Another is **High Peak Trail**, which follows the line of the former Cromford and High Peak Railway. This route takes in the stunning Derbyshire Dales countryside between Middleton Top and Parsley Hay. The **Manifold Trail**, another converted railway path, forms part of **National Route 54** between Hulme End and Waterhouses.

Useful maps and books (available from www.sustransshop.co.uk): *South Yorkshire & the Peak District cycle map; AA Cycling in the Midlands; Off-Road Trails & Quiet Lanes: Peak District; Cycling Traffic Free - Midlands and Peak District; and Cycling In The Peak District.*

CHAPTER II

PEAK DISTRICT "ROUGH-STUFF"

THE Peak District is second only, in England, to the Lake District as a pass-storming area. That is to say, Peakland possesses all the essentials for footpath exploration by bicycle: well-trodden surfaces, accessible starting and finishing points, relatively short journeys and convenience in crossing from valley-head to valley-head without traversing miles of main, and perhaps also suburban, roads.

All that I wrote about Lakeland pass-storming in "Northern England" applies equally to the Peak District. The footpaths enable the tourist to get closer to the mountains and hills, and by taking his bicycle with him the cyclist has a great advantage over the walker, who has, possibly, to tramp miles of less interesting country before reaching the hills, or is dependent upon public transport.

The Peak District crossings are, on the whole, easier and shorter than those of the Lake District. Moreover, the millstone grit when reduced to grains can become congealed by the weather and pounded by big boots into a smooth and quite usable surface, unlike the slatier stonier ways of Lakeland. A word of warning is required about Peakland. It is best to explore the tracks in mid-week and out of the summer season. The proximity of the district to Manchester and Sheffield makes it a regular haunt of week-enders and day walkers.

Similar cautions to those I gave on Lakeland are necessary about pass-storming in the Peak District. Heavy, even nailed, footgear is desirable, a companion or companions are safeguards, and plenty of food, a watch, compass and a 1-in. map are other necessities.

Most of the Peakland crossings are in the immediate vicinity of Kinder Scout, which has already been described on pages 46–47.

PEAKLAND CROSSINGS

Perhaps the easiest of all the major crossings in Peakland is that of **Edale Cross** (or Jacob's Ladder), between Edale and Hayfield. In reverse, this route provides a convenient route from the Lancashire and Cheshire towns to Edale and the Derwent Valley. It should not be attempted late in the evening, in bad weather, or after dark.

The route from Edale to Barber Booth and Jacob's Ladder follows a fair road. The deep lane which provides an alternative to the "Ladder" on its left side should be used. This is a stiff push of some hundreds of yards, and the track emerges on open moorland close to the stump of the boundary mark called Edale Cross (seen over a wall on the right). Edale Cross is the summit of the route, 1,750 ft. above sea level. A steep fall follows. On the right a succession of moorland bulwarks wind away to the plateau of Kinder Scout. After rainy weather the fan-shaped spray of Kinder Downfall can be seen. Soon the track divides. The right-hand one makes directly for Hayfield, by Tunstead Clough. The left-hand route is clearly the one to prefer. Soon the surface permits of riding, with care. Across a secondary valley to the left the shapely forms of Mount Famine and South Head can be seen, the culminations of a climbing ridge. Well over to the right lies Kinder Reservoir. Ahead, in a westerly direction, is the deep valley of the River Sett. Into this the track plunges by way of a tributary stream. Below the few buildings of Coldwell Clough there is a tolerable enough road, and the remaining miles into Hayfield lie through glades and between steep, green hills.

Edale Station to Hayfield, via Edale Cross, is 11 miles. About three hours should be allowed.

———

The most fascinating and perhaps the hardest of all the Peakland crossings is over **Ashop Head**, between Hayfield and the Snake Inn. This route passes within 1½ miles of the Kinder Plateau, and anyone who cares to risk the vigilance of keepers can hide his bicycle near the summit of the pass and walk to the edge of the plateau and round to the Kinder Downfall. The ascent from this side is hardly worth while, however, and a more sensible course is to walk from Rowland Cote youth hostel.

From Market Street, in Hayfield, the way first leads out by High Street and Kinder Road, and past Bank End Farm. The hills rise boldly as the highway—large stone setts at first and then much better—follows the bank of the River Kinder under a steep plantation (to the left) to within sight of the embankment of Kinder Reservoir. Here the path takes a sudden swing leftwards and climbs the steep hillside to the junction with a path that has come south-east from the Hayfield-Glossop road at Brook Houses.

The next section keeps on a ledge high above the Kinder Reservoir. Kinder Downfall and the whole flat head of Kinder Scout are well seen across the reservoir from this altitude. The path drops gently towards the head of the reservoir and then enters William Clough, a bare, austere hollow, out of which the track climbs steeply for about 1½ miles to Ashop Head, 1,761 ft. above sea level.

The track through William Clough was opened on May 29, 1897, after persistent efforts by the Peak District and Northern Counties Footpaths Preservation Society. The right to use it was established for ever.

The track, which has been going north-eastwards, takes a turn towards the east and enters the head of Ashop Clough. This is shallower than William Clough, and is served by many tributary streams. There is a freshness about Ashop Clough which is surprising after the west-side sterility. On the right the mountainside climbs sharply to The Edge, an impressive and sustained outcrop of gritstone fencing in the plateau. Soon a few small trees appear, and there is even a little stretch now and then when the bicycle can be ridden. A steep crest appears ahead, and below it a road. A little to the right lies the Snake Inn.

Hayfield to the Snake Inn, by Ashop Head, is 7½ miles. Say, about three hours.

The Snake Inn to Hayfield, by **Jagger's Clough**, completes a round of Kinder Scout. This crossing is little-known to cyclists. By using it the regular glutton for punishment could "box the Peak" in one long day.

From the Snake Inn the main Sheffield road should be followed south-eastward as far as Alport Bridge, near the 15th milestone from

Sheffield. The river should be crossed there, and the road running along the far side of the valley taken. This goes as a terrace road past Blackley Clough and Elmin Pits Farm before climbing sharply to the right beyond Crookstone Barn to cross the ridge near the course of a Roman road. The track then tends towards the right and goes, very steeply, into Jaggers Clough. This little valley is an epitome of a Pennine clough: steep, short, vee-shaped and with a brush of trees, whose foliage in autumn matches that of the bracken which covers much of this area.

There is a steep zig-zag climb out of the valley, and round a shoulder of hill. Thereafter comes an open descent to Clough Farm, on the main Edale road, a little east of Rowland Cote youth hostel.

Snake Inn to Clough Farm, by Jaggers Clough, 5 miles. About two hours.

Doctor's Gate, between Glossop and the Snake Inn, forms a parallel route to the Snake road described on pages 49–50. It is the most interesting historically of the Peakland crossings.

The easiest access to this track lies along a reservoir road going to the left off the Snake road below Shire Hill and beyond the 23rd milestone from Sheffield. This road leads down into Mossy Lee, where it joins another coming up the valley of the Shelf Brook. Here the way is rightward and up into the savage hill-country (all "Edges" and steep moorland crests) of Doctor's Gate.

This old track forms part of a Roman road, and the route was also used in prehistoric times. After leaving Crooked Clough (which heads north-east towards Bleaklow), the track crosses boulder-strewn moorland at a height of 1,686 ft. over Coldharbour Moor. The last section is down a narrow clough, which joins the Snake Road about 2½ miles above the Snake Inn. The whole of the track by Doctor's Gate is well marked.

Glossop to the Snake Inn, by Doctor's Gate, is 7 miles. About 2½ hours.

The longest moorland crossing in Peakland is **Cut Gate,** between the Flouch Inn (see page 19) and Ladybower. In relation to the lengths of the other tracks, and in one or two other particulars, it might be called, with many reservations, the Larig Ghru of the Peak District.

A long half-mile down the Sheffield road from the Flouch Inn, a track turns right into the moorland, and soon crosses the head of a reservoir by a bridge. Thereafter the track heads southward along the east side of Hingcliff to reach Mickleden Edge, above the stream in Bull Clough. (An alternative approach lies through Langsett and Upper Midhope, round the south side of the reservoir to a plantation, whence the track leads south-west to join the one from the Flouch Inn.)

The main track heads south on a ledge above Bull Clough, but where the clough goes rightward, in about a mile, the way is straight ahead along a passageway between peat banks which has a firm and sandy floor and can, indeed, be ridden in part. This is Cut Gate, the highest part of the track, 1,656 ft. above sea level.

The track next runs towards the south-west, leaving Margery Hill to the left, and descends, at first steadily but later in a series of zig-zags. This drop is very steep indeed, and from it there is a splendid prospect across the deeply-carved valley of the Upper Derwent at the edges and ridges of Bleaklow.

The descent continues between Bull Clough (another) and Cranberry Clough to the bridge at Slippery Stones, the site of a landslip. From here the tourist has the choice of travelling down either the west or east sides of the Derwent Valley Reservoirs as far as the foot of the second lake, where both roads join and keep to the west side. The east-side route is the shortest to this point. Flouch Inn to Ladybower, via Cutgate, is 12½ miles. About 4½ hours.

Chee Dale, between Buxton and Miller's Dale, forms perhaps the best short excursion in the limestone dales close to Buxton. The trip should only be attempted in a dry summer, however, because of the stepping stones at Chee Tor—covered by water and dangerous after rain.

From Buxton the Bakewell road should be followed down Ashwood Dale for 3 miles. As the road begins to climb Topley Pike (see page 42) a lane goes leftward through brushwood. This lane crosses the River Wye by a bridge close to the point where the

Buxton Branch of the former Midland Railway leaves the direct Manchester line. Quarries spoil the countryside hereabouts, but the natural beauty of the dale is already evident. The track goes rightward with the Wye and the railway, and then enters Chee Dale. The path becomes hemmed in by steep rocks and green dale-side and there is little room for it and the river. There is a great horseshoe bend at this point, making a most picturesque scene. The stepping stones do not cross the river but run round the edge of a bulging rock. Later the dale widens and the track is easier into Mijler's Dale.

Buxton to Miller's Dale, by Chee Dale, is about 7 miles. Time, say, 2½ hours.

Rough trails in the Peak District today

As Harold Briercliffe wrote this cycle route guide in 1949, many of the roads he mentions are now busier than they were and are not suitable for cycling today. Suggested alternative cycle routes, which are in the same location as Harold's original route are listed below.

The Pennine Bridleway is a 200-mile track for walkers, horse riders and mountain bikers. It follows old packhorse routes, drovers roads and newly created bridleways, the 120-mile southern section is open, including the 47-mile **Mary Towneley Loop**. The starting point for cyclists on the open part of the route is Middleton Top. Official opening of the full route, Derbyshire to Cumbria, is due in the summer of 2012.

Useful maps and books (available from www.sustransshop.co.uk): *South Yorkshire & the Peak District cycle map; Derbyshire & the Peak District (mountain-bike guide); High Peak Trails Mountain Bike Route Pack; Pennine Bridleway South (including Mary Towneley Loop)*

WHY DON'T YOU RIDE A Coventry-Eagle CYCLE I WISH I COULD!

WORKS ENTRANCE

Don't ask us what a giraffe's doing at a Works Entrance—we can't say. But by taking his advice you could be at YOUR job without hustle or bustle. And you could enjoy many happy carefree days on the open road.

Coventry·Eagle
CYCLES

THE COVENTRY-EAGLE CYCLE AND MOTOR CO. LTD., COVENTRY

CHAPTER III

CHESHIRE AND NORTH SHROPSHIRE

SOUTH of the River Mersey and west of the grand mass of Peakland, described in the two previous chapters, there stretches a district which provides excellent cycling. West Cheshire, North Shropshire and North Staffordshire are not, however, holidaymaking districts for cyclists. Few would spend even a long weekend amongst their lanes, unless they made Shrewsbury or Chester their headquarters. In all this country district there is at present only one youth hostel, in Delamere Forest. Shrewsbury and Chester have their hostels, as is right and proper, but otherwise Delamere is the only one.

Nevertheless, this is a traditional district for day trips awheel and for road-time trialing. If a circle of 40 miles radius is drawn around Knutsford on the map, it will take in Manchester, much of the industrial district upon which it depends, Liverpool and Merseyside and the Potteries—a population in all greater than any within a similar radius in the country, except for London.

Instead of sketching holiday tours and weekends, then, I will in this chapter indicate a number of the best destinations for day runs, giving where possible some indication of the distances from the industrial towns. Nearly all the places mentioned are within a day's out-and-home run of Manchester and its attendant towns, Bolton, Bury, Rochdale, Oldham, Ashton, Stalybridge, Hyde, Stockport and Leigh; of Liverpool, Birkenhead, Warrington, Wigan, St. Helens and Widnes and the Potteries. As the destinations and routes are intended mainly for the day rider, the week-ender and camper may make a more leisurely exploration at will.

While the district stretching south of the Mersey has no high ranges of mountains, only one notable river (the Dee) and a relative absence of woods, it has plenty of features geologically. Most of it is flat farming land, overlaying the new red sandstone, and where this crops up, as in the Peckforton, Delamere, Helsby and Alderley Edge districts, old domestic architecture as well as the scenery becomes interesting. The common impression that Cheshire and North Shropshire are flat and uninteresting is too superficial to be worth anything.

In this brief survey of the region outlined, I will begin at the north-west corner of Cheshire, in the Wirral district between the estuaries of the Mersey and the Dee, and work across the map from left to right, as in a book, until I reach the Severn near Atcham on one hand and the Potteries on the other. The district south of a line between the two latter places belongs to the Midlands proper, and will be treated in a further chapter.

THE WIRRAL

The Wirral Peninsula is about 20 miles long by about six miles wide, and extends north-westward from the vicinity of Chester (fully described in Cycling Guide No. 2, Wales). A busy main road connects Chester with Birkenhead, and from near Eastham, halfway along it, a spur road runs off to the south-west past Shotwick to cross the Dee in the industrialized area of Queensferry. This spur road is joined by the by-pass which skirts Chester on the north from near Fordsham, and both help to relieve the narrow streets of Chester from much traffic which would otherwise be thrust into their bottlenecks.

Chester, with its youth hostel and other accommodation and its intrinsic attractions, is the best starting-point from which to explore the Wirral. The tourist who wants to give the peninsula a hasty glance could follow the main road (Chester-Birkenhead, 15½ miles) and use the Mersey Tunnel to link up with the route described in Cycling Guide No. 1 by Southport to Preston for Lancaster and the Lake District.

Much more illuminating, however, would be to leave Chester by Northgate and Parkgate Road and then, soon after crossing the Queensferry road some seven miles out, turn left towards the Dee and the neat village of **Burton**, with its whitewashed cottages and sandstone footways. There are good views across the Dee estuary into Wales. Neston, the next village, has a few old houses and a cross, together with a sandstone church; but **Parkgate**, a little ahead, is a decayed little resort and a former packet station for Ireland. There is a good prospect across "the Sands o' Dee" and at the Welsh coast up to Point of Air. From the north-west end of the "front" at Parkgate a lane climbs back to the main road and runs on high ground past Heswall and through Thurstaston village and over Thurstaston Hill, the best of the Wirral viewpoints.

The descending road leads into the modern resort of West Kirkby, and then runs round to **Hoylake** over much built-up country. Hoylake is a popular resort, with good sea-bathing. Hilbre Point, to the west, is a mile from Hilbre Island, which can be reached across the sands on foot at low tide. The island is small and barren, and has little of interest.

From Hoylake the road runs inland through the bungalow town of Moreton, reaching the shore again near Leasowe Lighthouse. After about 1½ miles of straight going, there comes a road junction, left for the resort of New Brighton, and Seacombe and the ferries to Liverpool and right for **Birkenhead** and the Mersey Tunnel [now called the Queensway Tunnel].

By this route the distance between Chester and Birkenhead is about 32 miles. From Liverpool to Manchester along the new arterial road is 35 miles, and from the east end of the road (called "the East Lancashire Road") there are roads around the north side of Manchester for Rochdale and Oldham and for Halifax, Bradford, Huddersfield and Leeds (see Cycling Guide No. 1, Northern England).

Full round of the Wirral, Chester to Chester, is 47 miles.

DELAMERE FOREST

The Lancashire town of **Warrington,** on the north side of the Mersey, makes a good starting-point for an exploration of the Helsby Hill and Delamere Forest districts (Liverpool, 18; Manchester, 18; Wigan, 12½; London, 181½ miles).

Just south of Warrington, great roads part, one going leftwards to Knutsford, the Potteries and London; another making straight ahead for Tarporley and Shrewsbury; and one other going rightward alongside the Mersey for Chester and North Wales. The last is the one to follow.

From Walton Hall the Chester road runs through undulating country past Daresbury to Preston Brook, and near Halton Station crosses the Weaver Navigation Canal and the River Weaver. These come through a green vale from Northwich.

Frodsham, the next town, is a straggling place built on two hills. There are opportunities here for meals.

Just south of Frodsham, in the outlying suburb of Netherton, a fork-road swings leftwards. On either hand at this point are bold sandstone cliffs. The one to the south-west, **Helsby Hill**, is the most noteworthy, and from it there is a splendid view of the Mersey Estuary and of Delamere Forest.

The fork road climbs steadily through a quiet and wooded district, passing east of Common Side to a crossroads west of Birch Hill. Next the way is rightwards—still along B5393—and on to Rangersbank. Here the way is straight ahead for nearly a mile. Then after a dip to a brook comes the railway and next a crossroads.

Here left again. This is the western edge of Delamere Forest. Near the railway bridge is "Fox Howl," the Delamere Forest youth hostel.

Beyond the bridge the forest proper is entered, making a delightful up-and-down run to the crossroads at Hatchmere. Refreshments are obtainable hereabouts, while the mere itself, to the north of the crossing, is a charming little sheet. From Hatchmere a series of lanes run eastward past Norley and Brinn into **Northwich.** (Altrincham, 12½; Chester, 17½; Congleton, 15½; Crewe, 15; Macclesfield, 18; Manchester, 21; Nantwich, 16; Shrewsbury, 45; Warrington, 11½; Whitchurch, 25; London, 170 miles.)

This run from Warrington via Delamere Forest to Northwich is about 24 miles long. More details about Northwich are given on page 81.

DEESIDE, PECKFORTON
AND BEESTON CASTLE

From **Chester** the tourist can do a good round taking in the River Dee at Eaton Hall and visiting Malpas, the Peckforton Hills and Beeston Castle.

The Wrexham road must be followed first for 4 miles to a lodge on the left. Here the private grounds of Eaton Hall are entered, and an avenue followed to the hall, seat of the Duke of Westminster. East of the hall, the River Dee is crossed at a very pleasant reach at the Iron Bridge.

The grounds are left near the picturesque village of Aldford, and then route follows a pleasant lane, travelling by Churton to Farndon, where the Dee is crossed by a bridge into **Holt**. The bridge is a fine old structure, well worth cycling to see.

Returning into Farndon, the road going west should be followed for a short way. Soon a lane to the right goes off this, and this lane should be taken past Stretton and Tilston to the quaint township of **Malpas**, on high ground.

From the town the route going north-east past Malpas Station is followed by Hampton Heath to the church near Gallantry Bank. Here the way leads rightwards along the picturesque east flank of the Peckforton Hills, which rise in a brown, evergreen-topped ridge to the left, with a glimpse of the private residence of Peckforton Castle. Soon afterwards **Beeston Castle** rises on the left, and can be reached by climbing a short hill.

The castle was built in 1220, was besieged more than once in the Civil War, and in 1646 was dismantled. The ruins are extensive, and the castle itself is entered by rough steps to a gateway on the west side. Two sides of the keep are on the edge of a precipice composed of old red sandstone. From the castle there is a splendid view across the Dee and the Mersey, and from the Welsh Hills to the Peak District.

From Beeston Castle it is an easy run through the old coaching town of **Tarporley,** where meals are obtainable, and by Tarvin back to Chester, making a total distance for the round of some 40 miles.

BARTON BRIDGE TO FRODSHAM

The tourist who has followed the route north of Manchester by Agecroft to Barton Bridge (see Cycling Guide No. 1, Northern England), or who aims at reaching Shrewsbury from Bolton or Blackburn (and from the Yorkshire Dales or the Trough of Bowland), can by-pass Manchester and miss the busy Manchester-Chester road by following a delightful lane route through North Cheshire and into Shropshire.

This first goes over the Manchester Ship Canal and turns rightwards for Crofts Bank. Here the way is right again, and then follows a sequence of left-right-left-right turns through the suburb of Davyhulme before emerging at Flixton Station. There is more of the left-right action along the road to Carrington, where the farming country on the south side of the River Mersey is gained. From here a lane route wanders across the levels past Partington to the twin villages of Heatley and Warburton (where an alternative route from Bolton through Leigh comes in over a bridge across the Manchester Ship Canal). A right turn in Heatley leads up to the old-world village of **Lymm**, just off the busy Altrincham-Warrington road.

Lymm makes a pleasant half-day run from the South Lancashire industrial towns. In the old village is a market cross standing on steps cut in rock. The chief charm of Lymm, however, is the Dam, a sheet of water commencing close to the modern church on the main road. There is a pleasant woodland walk along the west side of the water for about 25 miles.

From the new village of Lymm a by-road route runs generally south-west past Grappenhall Lodge and Stretton to Preston-on-the-Hill and the main Warrington-Frodsham road described previously. From Barton Bridge to Frodsham by this route is about 25 miles.

BARTON BRIDGE TO SHREWSBURY

Another useful route from Barton Bridge leads across country to Shrewsbury. This leaves the previous route at Heatley Warburton, and strikes southwards, crossing the Bridgwater Canal, and then climbing up to Broomedge, on the Altrincham-Warrington road. Beyond this point (where the way at the crossroads is straight ahead) the tourist enters the pleasant district around High Legh, and continues over the Knutsford-Warrington road (part of the great highway between London and Glasgow) into the Arley neighbourhood. Arley Park, to the right, is worth exploration. Its speciality is rhyming signposts. The road-forks beyond this point are confusing, but it is best to make for **Great Budworth,** which has a church on a hill and some half-timbered houses. Budworth Mere, to the west, is less accessible than **Pickmere**, to the east, the latter being a more-than-popular week-ending haunt.

From Great Budworth it is not difficult to find the way into **Northwich**, three miles to the south. The town is a salt-mining and pumping centre, and possesses works ancillary to the process. All along its main street, carrying the Manchester-Chester main road, the most exceptional house subsidences can be found, bringing bedroom windows level with the pavements and putting walls out of perpendicular.

From Northwich the main Chester road must be followed for 5½ miles to Crabtree Green, where a left turn leads through woodland country to Cotebrook and Tarporley (see page 79).

Tarporley can be missed by going left at Cotebrook by Eaton to Four Lane Ends; a slightly shorter route.

Beyond Four Lane Ends the route leads past the lane for Beeston Castle (see page 79) and on through picturesque upland country— very little populated on the whole—to Ridley Green, then passing Cholmondley Castle and Park to the west before going by Bickley Moss into the market town of **Whitchurch**, with its halts for cyclists (fuller details in Cycling Guide No. 2, Wales).

Of the two routes between Whitchurch and Shrewsbury, the more easterly one through Preston Brockhurst is the most interesting, although slightly longer. It passes over the open stretch of Prees Heath and close to the romantic region of Hawkstone Park, traversing a pretty little pass. Preston Brockhurst has a 17th-century hall, and at 16½ miles from Shrewsbury the route passes Battlefield, a modern village just south-east of the site of the Battle of Shrewsbury (1403). The church commemorates the battle.

Shrewsbury is entered by St. Michaels Street and Castle Foregate. Full particulars of the city will be found in Cycling Guide No. 2.

The alternative route between Whitchurch and Shrewsbury passes, about halfway, the attractive village-town of Wem, its main point of interest.

From Barton Bridge to Shrewsbury by this route is about 65 miles.

MANCHESTER TO WELLINGTON

The tourist making for Wellington (for West Shropshire, South Wales and the Wye Valley) from Manchester will find that a pleasant and fairly direct route is to take the Chester road—second only to the Alderley Edge road as the Manchester cyclists' favourite—through Altrincham (western outskirts), down the bank at Bowden, and over North Cheshire's own stream, the Bollin, then up Bucklow Hill to the modern village at its head. Here the way is leftward by A5034 along a road which passes closely on the right the charming sheet called The Mere. (This lake gives its name to the village less than a mile west where the London-Glasgow highway crosses the Manchester-Chester road— one of the busiest crossings in England, a Crewe of the British highways system.) This side road soon joins the London-Glasgow road (here called A50), and then enters **Knutsford**.

This old-world town, which the main road traverses, is the "Cranford" of the novel by Mrs. Gaskell, who is buried in the Unitarian Chapel grounds. Knutsford has several places catering for travellers, and its grimmest building is the old Cheshire County Jail. On May Days Knutsford celebrates thoroughly.

Some pleasant travelling through avenues and meadows— reminiscent of Hertfordshire—leads along the main road south for 2 miles to a fork. Here the way is rightward, away from the main road and along a pleasant secondary highway, passing, on the left, the neat, compact village of Lower Peover (pronounced "Peever"), and then entering more open country until the road—B5081— reaches **Middlewich**. The River Dane is crossed just before entering the town. Middlewich is an historic place, now partly industrialized.

From the town a less interesting highway runs south-west to **Nantwich**, a town with plenty of "magpie" (i.e., black and white) architecture. There are catering houses here—a halt might be desirable, because calling-places become fewer for some miles. From Nantwich a quiet and undulating highway goes through the pretty village of Hankelow and into the small, old townlet of Audlem, afterwards continuing into Adderley, in Shropshire, and **Market Drayton**, an old town.

About 1½ miles farther on is the hill-top house called Mount

Pleasant, where a lane forking rightwards forms a useful connection by way of Mill Green, Childs Ercall, Eaton-on-Tern, Great Bolas and Waters Upton, with the main road from Whitchurch to Wellington, near Crudgington. Ahead now the hogsback of The Wrekin can be seen and the route reaches a crossroads near **Wellington** on the London-Holyhead main road. Manchester-Wellington is 67 miles. For continuation to Bridgnorth southward see pages 109–110.

The foregoing route can be joined from the east side of Manchester by travelling from Longsight along Slade Lane to Kingsway, a modern highway built in the 1920s, to Cheadle Green, most popular rendezvous of Manchester clubmen. Here the way is rightwards along Cheadle's main street, and then left opposite the church for Handforth and Wilmslow, a suburbanized route. To the right, just off the Wilmslow-Altrincham road, is the Clarion Club House, at Oversley Ford, a friendly cyclists' haunt, replacing a former one at Handforth.

After Wilmslow the jutting form of **Alderley Edge** can be seen rising to the south-east. There are wide views from the Edge and much good rambling country in the vicinity, as well as Copper Mines to explore for the adventurous. The Edge rises to 650 ft. above sea level.

Just before the railway bridge in the suburb of Alderley Edge a highway strikes rightward for Chelford (the main road continues southward to Congleton), passing on the left in half a mile the quaint old moated house called Chorley Hall, dating from 1420. At Chelford this by-road crosses the Knutsford-Macclesfield highway and then runs through pleasant wooded country not unfamiliar to time-trialists, down and up the dips of Badger Bank and Jodrell Bank, before passing Twemlow Pump and entering Holmes Chapel, on the London-Glasgow highway. The latter is followed southward for a short way, and then a right turn taken beyond Brereton Green (where there is an old inn) for **Sandbach,** an old town with two Saxon crosses, fine examples of their kind, tucked away in a corner of the square. Beyond Sandbach an urbanized highway leads into **Crewe,** famous for its railway junction and workshops, and then onwards into Nantwich (see opposite). From Manchester to Nantwich (for Wellington or Shrewsbury), by Holmes Chapel, is 38 miles.

ALDERLEY TO NEWCASTLE-UNDER-LYME

The rider who uses the part of the foregoing route which lies between Manchester and Alderley Edge will want to know more about the main road continuing southward to Congleton and Newcastle-under-Lyme. Although this is a more direct route between Manchester and Newcastle-under-Lyme, for Birmingham or London, it is less used by heavy and through traffic than the wider, more modern, road through Holmes Chapel.

From Alderley Edge town it climbs over a westerly prolongation of the Edge itself, and then reaches Nether Alderley, where there is a fine roadside barn, with a mossy stone roof, in a depression on the left, and an old-fashioned row of cottages on the right leading down a cul-de-sac to the village church. The road maintains its southerly direction, skirting on the left the grounds of Alderley Hall, a seat of the Stanley family. At Monks Heath, 3 miles from Alderley Edge, the Knutsford-Macclesfield road is met at a crossroads. More of the characteristically pretty East Cheshire scenery follows as the highway undulates past Capesthorne Hall, on the right, famous for its rhododendrons, and drops to a charming S-bend between two minor meres on the right and the larger Redesmere on the left. The latter is one of the largest of the Cheshire lakes, and can be approached more closely down the next lane on the left.

Through the hamlet of Siddington the highway keeps its pleasant surroundings and soon it reaches, on the left, the prettiest perhaps of the Cheshire black-and-white churches, that of Marton. The interest is less pronounced as the highway approaches Congleton. (Down a side lane on the left is the once-deserted village of Havannah.)

Congleton is reached by way of a steep descent which until recently was adorned with a "land lighthouse." If the drop is steep, it is in no way exceptional, and the need for the "lighthouse" was always questionable. The town has some quaint inns and old houses and was formerly notorious for its bull-baiting.

The way out of the town first runs westward, and then resumes its true direction towards the south. The bold hill to the north-east is Bosley Cloud, while to the east the long ridge of Mow Cop may be seen. Three miles south of Congleton, on the left, stands

Moreton Old Hall, a place which is well worth a visit. An admission charge is made, but there are concessions to members of the Cyclists' Touring Club and the National Cyclists' Union. The hall is in the familiar black-and-white style. Mow Cop, rising to the east, is surmounted by sham ruins and has hill-top quarries.

The road continues through Scholar Green, and beyond the crossroads of Red Bull enters Staffordshire, and immediately begins to climb the mile-long hill of Talke. Towards the top of this the Glasgow road comes in from Knutsford, and thereafter as far as Newcastle-under-Lyme the way is dingy as the western edge of the Potteries is traversed. Alderley to Newcastle, is 23 miles.

NEWCASTLE-UNDER-LYME (Birmingham, 43; Coventry, 58; Leicester, 58; Lichfield, 31; Stafford, 16½; London, 147 miles) is the least objectionable of the Potteries towns, and is easily traversed by the cyclist bound for the South from Manchester.

EAST CHESHIRE

There is far more to see in East Cheshire than can be brought within the scope of this chapter, which can only hint at some of the attractions of the district. Places between the Manchester-Congleton road and the Manchester-Glossop road which are desirable day-run destinations from the Manchester district include: **Prestbury**, north-west of Macclesfield, an old-world village, with a fine church and a Norman chapel, an old half-timbered vicarage, and an ancient inn; **Gawsworth**, south-west of Macclesfield, with an old hall, church and vicarage and the grave of "Maggotty Johnson," an 18th-century wit, whose rhyming epitaph is most thorough; the whole hill region south of Disley in the direction of Rainow; the valley of the River Goyt south of Marple, near Stockport; the breezy roads across Werneth Low in the same district; and the neighbourhood of Pott Shrigley, north-east of Macclesfield.

All these deserve the detailed exploration which can be undertaken by the resident in a district, but not so easily by the tourist with his limited time.

Cycling in Cheshire and North Shropshire today

As Harold Briercliffe wrote this cycle route guide in 1949, many of the roads he mentions are now busier than they were and are not suitable for cycling today. Suggested alternative cycle routes, from Sustrans, which are in the same location as Harold's original route are listed below. To devise your own detailed route and map in the region, go to www.sustrans.org.uk.

National Cycle Network Route 45 runs from **Chester** down to **Ironbridg**e in Shropshire, a distance of around 70 miles. The route meanders mainly along minor roads through some beautiful countryside via Whitchurch, and crosses some of the Cheshire Cycleway. You could start or finish at **Ironbridge Gorge**, the place recognised as the birthplace of the Industrial Revolution, symbolised by the first iron bridge, which was built over the River Severn in 1779. The gorge and its bridge are now a World Heritage Site.

The **Cheshire Cycleway** is marked as **Regional Route 70** of the National Cycle Network and is a circular route around the county. The route is 176 miles long and takes you along quiet lanes to visit some of Cheshire's gems. You can visit Chester, pop up to Parkgate, and then go across the Cheshire plain. To the east the route delivers fine views from high up in the Gritstone Hills (just inside the Peak National Park).

Useful maps and books (available from www.sustransshop.co.uk): *Cycling Traffic Free – Midlands and Peak District*. Also, visit *www.cheshirecycleway.co.uk*.

CHAPTER IV

EAST OF THE PENNINES

THE parts of Yorkshire, Derbyshire and Nottinghamshire lying east of the Pennines have fewer places of interest to the cyclist than those to the west. A large amount of the area is given over to coal mining, and the colliery district spreads more and more to the east as time goes on. There are, however, many isolated corners in which the predominating influence of mining is overcome by historical interest or by the survival of some leafy landscapes amidst the pit shafts.

Of the remaining woodlands, the best known are The Dukeries, the district around Worksop which at one time contained the seats of several dukes, and still retains its parkland character. Even here, however, the new pits are creeping farther eastward. Some of the parks are traversed by public roads, others have drives along which cycling is permitted, while a few are completely closed to tourists.

The whole of The Dukeries can be visited in a long weekend. Riders from Lancashire or Yorkshire making for Lincolnshire or East Anglia, or Londoners heading northward can gain a satisfactory impression of the district without deviating greatly from the direct routes through it.

THE DUKERIES

Sheffield stands directly in the way of the Manchester or Liverpool rider making for The Dukeries, Sherwood and the Eastern Counties. Luckily, the tourist can skirt the city fairly easily by a hilly but interesting route to the south.

The starting-point is the road junction of **Whaley Bridge,** on the Manchester-Buxton road, in North Derbyshire (see page 40).

From Whaley Bridge the road through Chapel-en-le-Frith and over Mam Tor should be taken to Castleton, as described in reverse on page 47. Then the Vale of Hope must be followed past Hope to Hathersage (10½), described fully on page 52. After this dale village comes a steady climb of 3 miles to Fox House, passing the "Surprise

View" and the Toad Rock. Here the way is straight on, in a south-easterly direction, to a road fork, where left to the exposed moorland crossroads of **Owler Bar** (17). Next the route goes straight on again into the old-fashioned village of **Holmesfield**, typically Pennine in its hilltop situation. About 1½ miles south-eastwards, in the picturesque Cordwell Valley, lies the small youth hostel of Peakley Hill.

The through route continues past Dronfield Woodhouse, and then drops to Dronfield, on the Chesterfield-Sheffield road. This is crossed and another climb follows into Coal Aston, after which the route becomes involved as it threads its way along secondary roads past Marsh Lane into **Eckington**. Next the route skirts, to the right hand, the park of Renishaw Hall, seat of the Sitwell family, in a busy mining area, and climbs past Renishaw village into the village of Barlborough, with its creamy stone walls and red tiles, symbols of the charm once common in this now-industrialized area. The main road onwards skirts the mining townlet of Clowne, and then approaches the newer built-up area of Creswell. Less than a mile beyond a railway bridge, down the second turning on the left, a side road runs along a little dale and passes the long, bold line of **Creswell Crags**. These are on a surprising limestone "fault," scenically well worth cycling to see, and important for the pre-historic finds in their caves. The side road emerges on the Cuckney-Worksop road (36) opposite one of the entrances to **Welbeck Park**. It is usually possible for cyclists (not motorists) to enter the park by asking the gatekeeper's permission. The Abbey is at present being used as a military college.

The road through the park skirts Welbeck Abbey, and then plunges into a string of tunnels, lit by shafts from the park above, and passing below the Great Lake of Welbeck. It is an eerie experience to ride through the tunnels. Further on a by-road runs north and then east through an agricultural part of the park before emerging on the Budby-Worksop road on Sparken Hill.

Here the tourist should turn right towards the south and traverse the woodlands past Scotland Farm to a crossroads just beyond a bridge. By going leftward here the pretty village of **Carburton** can be traversed, and then the grounds of the former Clumber House entered (National Trust property). Soon after the gate, a right fork leads towards the site of the house. A short way along, however, it is best to turn rightward, after passing along the north-west side of a narrow lake, and reach a bridge, from which there is one of the best views in The Dukeries. Next, a return to the approach road must follow. By going leftward near the lovely church, the only remnant of Clumber House, which was pulled down in the 1930s, the 3-mile-long drive called Lime Tree Avenue can be reached and followed northeastwards to the Apley Head Gate and "Clumber House," on the Blyth-Ollerton road. By going rightward down this latter road for 3 miles a crossroads is gained. Here the way is rightward through the grounds of Thoresby Hall, and so by the north side of Budby and through Cuckney to the starting-point opposite the gate to Welbeck Abbey and near Creswell Crags. The complete route from the gates and back is about 17 miles.

The outline Dukeries tour covers sketchily most of the large parks in the area. It also avoids, as much as possible, the new colliery districts. There are no youth hostels in The Dukeries, but accommodation can be sought in the smaller centres, carefully avoiding the rawer mining villages. Cuckney, Budby, Ollerton and Edwinstowe all offer possibilities, while a little farther afield Worksop, Tuxford and Retford are all likely places. A popular cyclists' rendezvous is Blyth, 6 miles north-east of Worksop.

South of The Dukeries proper lies the part of Sherwood Forest associated with the legendary band of Robin Hood. This district has been gathered up by the coalfield to a greater extent than The Dukeries, and its "sights" can be only approached through the new pit villages. These are much less grimy than the older ones, but nevertheless the average tourist will choose to avoid them.

East of the Nottingham-Ollerton-Bawtry road there has been little penetration by the pits, and between this highway and the Great North Road from Newark to Bawtry there are several old-world and picturesque villages. A notable one is Laxton, about 3 miles south-west of Tuxford, where the Middle Ages survives in its "strip" system of cultivation.

Bilhaugh Forest, once much wider but now confined to glades

north-west of Ollerton, is a fragment of old Sherwood, while west of this lie the remains of the Major Oak.

Further south, about halfway between Mansfield and Nottingham, stands Newstead Abbey, in a pretty, lake-dotted valley. The park is open to cyclists, and the abbey may be visited also. It is owned by the City of Nottingham, and is well looked after. The Abbey includes a Byron Museum.

The Mansfield-Nottingham road keeps to high ground and runs through detached portions of woodland. Some five miles from Mansfield a fork to the right leads down by Papplewick and past Bestwood, forming an alternative route to the main road.

The cyclist who has reached the entrance to Welbeck Abbey, as on page 88, and who wishes to see a corner of The Dukeries while making for the Eastern Counties, can travel south-eastward past Cuckney and Budby into Ollerton, for Kelham and Newark, or from Cuckney past Thoresby Park (as described in reverse on page 89), Bothamsall, Markham Moor, East Markham, Darlton and Dunham into Lincoln.

The cyclist from the Leeds-Bradford district making for The Dukeries would be well advised to go through Wakefield and then follow the Doncaster road, which avoids the adjacent colliery villages in the main. From Doncaster the way lies southward through Tickhill and Oldcoates.

Cycling East of the Pennines today

As Harold Briercliffe wrote this cycle route guide in 1949, many of the roads he mentions are now busier than they were and are not suitable for cycling today. Suggested alternative cycle routes, from Sustrans, which are in the same location as Harold's original route are listed below. To devise your own detailed route and map in the region, go to www.sustrans.org.uk.

The National Cycle Network Route 6 runs for approximately 68 miles between **Derby** and **Sheffield** in the Peak District area. The majority of this route is traffic-free, including a converted railway path from **Blidworth** to **Sherwood Forest**, where cycle paths guide you through the famous forest.

Useful maps and books (available from www.sustransshop.co.uk): *South Yorkshire & the Peak District cycle map; AA Cycling in the Midlands; Cycling Traffic Free – Midlands and Peak District.*

EVER READY

REGD. TRADE MARK

Cycle Lamps and Batteries

When cycling at night let Ever Ready be your guide. There is no more convenient and trouble-free form of cycle lighting than an Ever Ready Battery in an Ever Ready Lamp.

CHAPTER V

THE WEST-CENTRAL MIDLANDS

THE huge modern city of Birmingham dominates the district between the undulating wolds of Leicestershire and the Shropshire hills. Birmingham, the Black Country to the west, the Potteries to the north, and Wolverhampton and Coventry, form such strong features that the tourist might well believe that amongst such industrialism there is little to see. This is quite a wrong impression however, for while there is little enough scope for long tours, the cyclist making across the Midlands for more favoured parts, or seeking a weekend in sylvan surroundings, or even looking out for a suitable venue for a day run, will find a great deal of attraction.

West of the Potteries, around Maer, there is a fresh, sandy belt of hills, and nearby, close to the polluted River Trent, is the little patch of Needwood Forest. Further eastward rises the knot of rock scenery in Charnwood Forest. Lichfield is a fine old town, too.

The most striking scenery, however, lies to the northwest and west of Birmingham. Notable here is the wooded peak of the Wrekin and the gorge of the River Severn as it flows between Atcham and Bewdley. The relics of early industrialism about Ironbridge are themselves of interest, while the hill ranges of Wenlock Edge and around Cleobury Mortimer are full of byways which reveal nooks and corners of the greatest charm.

NEWCASTLE-UNDER-LYME TO COVENTRY

The rider making from Manchester towards Coventry (for London) or Birmingham can see quite a good deal of interest along the main route given herewith, and by branching leftward or rightward could get more comprehensive impressions of the area.

Newcastle-under-Lyme (see page 85) is left by High Street, Cheapside, Penkhull Street and London Road, and after 4 miles the pits and the potteries are left behind as the road passes, on the right, the pleasure resort of Trentham Gardens, and undulates down the Trent Valley into **Stone** (8½), a country town with a long, narrow main street.

The next few miles are amongst the pleasantest between Manchester and London by this route. Through the "model" village of Sandon, grouped around its green, the road runs alongside Sandon Park (left of the road). The next village, Weston-on-Trent, straggles along the highway. Beyond the railway a road goes rightward, climbs a steep hill and reaches Stafford (see page 97) in about five miles.

The going remains pleasant into Great Haywood. To the west, and worth a divergence, lies the long causeway and bridge built to enable Queen Elizabeth to travel readily from Chartley Castle to Cannock Chase.

The next large place is **Rugeley** (Newcastle-under-Lyme, 23½; Birmingham, 23½; Lichfield, 7½; Stafford, 9½; London, 124 miles), a manufacturing town with the remains of a castle, and once notorious for its associations with Palmer, the poisoner.

North-east of Rugeley stretches the remaining fragment of the old forest of Needwood, still a rural district of dark woodlands and timber-framed houses. **Abbots Bromley**, 6 miles from Rugeley, is the natural headquarters of this region. In September there takes place in the town a Horn Dance, based on a ritual reproduction of an old-time hunt. The best part of the forest lies within Bagot's Park, between Abbots Bromley and the River Dove. There is a convenient youth hostel for this district at Wandon, 2½ miles south of Rugeley.

From Rugeley there are two ways into Lichfield, one by Brereton and Longdon, which is hilly and rural as well as direct, and another through Armitage, which is more level, used by the lorry traffic and longer. Both rejoin at a hilltop about one mile north-west of Lichfield.

LICHFIELD. M.D., Fri. E.C.D., Wed. (Newcastle-under-Lyme, 31; Ashbourne, 26½; Banbury, 52; Birmingham, 16; Buxton, 46½; Chester, 65½; Coventry, 27½; Derby, 24; Leicester, 37; Manchester, 67½; Northampton, 54½; Nottingham, 39½; Oxford, 74½; Stafford, 17; Stamford, 68; Uttoxeter, 18; Warrington, 65½; Warwick, 32½; London, 116 miles.) Lichfield is mostly famous for its cathedral, with three graceful spires. Dr. Johnson was born here, and his birthplace is now a museum. Although much through traffic thunders along its main street, the modest explorer will find in

Lichfield many quiet corners. (There is a youth hostel at Lichfield.)

Three miles farther south A446 crosses the line of Watling Street, numbered A5 in the Ministry of Transport's classification. By going left along Watling Street, a shorter, straighter route to London is available, by Atherstone to Weedon Beck. This route is lacking in interest, and the tourist is recommended to follow the road described.

Once across Watling Street, the Coventry road begins to climb in a lonely region, passing Bassett's Pole, and then descends gradually into **Coleshill,** entered by a bridge and a steep climb up the main street. Near the top of the hill the Nuneaton-Birmingham road crosses the route.

The next few miles are straight, level and leafy, and then, after the road from Shrewsbury skirting Birmingham on the north-east has joined the route and a railway bridge has been crossed, the important crossroads of **Stonebridge** is reached. Here in the early days of club cycling the wheeling gallants of Birmingham and Coventry were wont to gather. Stonebridge is 10 miles from Birmingham and 8½ miles from Coventry.

By going straight ahead at Stonebridge, the cyclist travelling from the north and making for the Cotswolds, Devon and Cornwall, can use the pleasantest and least-industrialized of linking routes through the Midlands. The route traverses undulating wooded country, reaching **Kenilworth,** a scattered town most noted for its castle, which has a Norman keep dating from 1180, and for a water-splash nearby which provides a refreshing interlude on a hot summer's day.

Through more rural scenes the route enters the health resort of **Leamington Spa,** nowadays concerned with light industry as well, and next comes to Warwick, the architectural gem of the district. Here, there is a 14th-century, castle, with Guy of Warwick's Tower, 128 ft. high and with stout walls, and also Caesar's Tower, 147 ft. high. Lord Leycester's Hospital is a 14th-century half-timbered building. There is also an old bridge across the River Avon and the East and West Gates across the high main street.

A tree-lined highway, rising and falling in well-engineered curves, leads to Stratford-on-Avon, 8½ miles from Warwick.

STRATFORD-ON-AVON. M.D., Mon., Wed., Frid. E.C.D., Thurs. (Lichfield—by Warwick—41; Banbury, 20; Bath, 73½; Birmingham, 24; Broadway, 15; Cheltenham, 30½; Chipping Norton, 22; Cirencester, 40½; Coventry, 19; Droitwich, 22; Evesham, 14½; Gloucester, 38½; Kidderminster, 30; Moreton-in-the-Marsh, 17; Northampton, 39½; Oxford, 39½; Rugby, 25½; Shrewsbury, 64½; Worcester, 25; London, 91.) The birthplace of Shakespeare—otherwise it might have remained an unpretentious country town beside the quiet Avon. From Stratford a delightful hillfoot road leads past Mickleton, Broadway and Winchcombe to Cheltenham, for the upland route by Stroud to Bath, and to the West Country (see Cycling Guide No. 4, South-West England).

The London-bound tourist should turn left at Stonebridge and rise gently to **Meriden.** Here is one of the reputed "centres" of England. On Meriden Green, to the left of the road and now perilously close to its busy traffic stream, stands the Cyclists' War Memorial, a plain obelisk unveiled on May 21, 1921, to commemorate the cyclists who died in the 1914-18 war.

The Coventry road, a broad modern highway, mounts to Allesley, and then enters the city. A by-pass going rightward at Allesley avoids the congested streets of Coventry.

From Coventry the main road to London goes through Dunchurch, avoids Daventry by a by-pass (there is a youth hostel at Badby, a little south-west), and then passes through Weedon and Towcester (to the west of which is Astwell Castle Youth Hostel), Stony Stratford, Dunstable and St. Albans. This is a wide, undulating route, the busiest in Britain for long-distance lorry traffic.

An alternative route between the Midlands and London is given in reverse on pages 154–155.

NEWCASTLE-UNDER-LYME TO GLOUCESTER

The Lancashire or Yorkshire cyclist requiring a fast main route to the West Country and one avoiding the larger Midland towns, should first of all make for Newcastle-under-Lyme and continue to the northern outskirts of Stone, as described on page 93. Here a road forks right and continues southward to Stafford.

STAFFORD. M.D., Fri. and Sat. E.C.D., Wed. (Newcastle-under-Lyme, 16½; Ashbourne, 26; Birmingham, 27; Burton-on-Trent, 26; Chester, 48½; Derby, 32½; Lichfield, 17; Liverpool, 68; Manchester, 53; Shrewsbury, 31; Warrington, 51; Wolverhampton, 16½; Worcester, 37; London, 133 miles.)

An old town with modern electrical and salt industries, amongst others. Some half-timbered domestic architecture remains. Its streets are narrow, but the place is easily traversed.

Just south of Stafford, a road forks left (A455) for Cannock and Birmingham and Coventry. About five miles from the county town this road begins to travel across Cannock Chase, a large area of woodland not completely spoilt by coal-mining, denudation and conifer-planting. Huntington, the next village, is devoted to mining and then the road passes through the unlovely hill-top town of CANNOCK (Newcastle-under-Lyme, 26½; Birmingham, 17; Coventry, 33; Lichfield, 9; Shrewsbury, 32½; Stafford, 10; Walsall, 8½, Wolverhampton, 9, London, 125 miles) and descends to the Watling Street. By going straight on here Birmingham can be reached through Walsall. A left turn along Watling Street leads by Brownhills to New Oscott, and through the eastern suburbs of Birmingham by Castle Bromwich to Stonebridge, passing Fort Dunlop. At Stonebridge the route between Newcastle-under-Lyme and Coventry, described on pages 93–94, is encountered. The Cannock route misses Birmingham also, and forms an alternative to the Lichfield-Coleshill run. It is, however, less picturesque than the latter.

Cannock Chase is a worthy venue for a Midland weekend run. A useful base for exploration is **Wandon** Youth Hostel, south-east of Rugeley (see page 94).

From Stafford the main route between Manchester and the south-west runs across open farming country past Penkridge, and at Gailey (where there is an old-established cyclists' calling-place to the left at Gailey Wharf) crosses the Watling Street, and soon enters

Wolverhampton (Newcastle-under-Lyme, 33).

Leave by way of Worcester Street and Penn Road, and in 5½ miles reach Himley, with its old hall. This district is on the edge of the industrial area, and after a right fork beyond Himley it runs through an interesting undulating countryside into Kidderminster. All the district to the east, between Halesowen in the south and Wolverhampton in the north, is best avoided by the touring cyclist. The Clent Hills, however, between Halesowen and Kidderminster, form a high, wooded region, worth exploring carefully by the local cyclist.

Leave **Kidderminster** (48½) by Worcester Road, and go by Crossway Green and into the crossroads village of **Ombersley**, a very picturesque place, full of half-timbered houses. A mile ahead the road reaches a descent which has a fine prospect down the Severn Valley.

Through parkland the road next enters the important county town of Worcester (Newcastle-under-Lyme, 67½).

Worcester should be left by High Street, College Street and Sidbury. Then the Tewkesbury road undulates by the pretty village of Kempsey and on through Severn Stoke into Tewkesbury.

TEWKESBURY M.D., Wed. E.C.D., Thurs. (Birminghan 42; Broadway, 16; Bristol, 46; Cheltenham, 9; Evesham 13; Newcastle-under-Lyme, 83; Oxford, 51; London, 104 miles.

A most picturesque place, largely because of the numbe: of half-timbered houses. There is a fine abbey church and the situation of the town close to the confluence of the Severn and the Avon, and amidst the water meadows, is a fine one. The remainder of the route into Gloucester is level and winding.

GLOUCESTER. M.D., Mon. and Sat. E.C.D., Thurs. (Abergavenny, 39½; Aberystwyth, 110½; Burford, 32; Bath, 38; Birmingham, 53; Bournemouth, 99; Bristol, 35; Cardiff, 56; Cheltenham, 9; Chepstow, 28½; Great Malvern, 25½; Hereford, 31; Lichfield, 69; Monmouth, 24½; Newcastle-under-Lyme, 94; Oxford, 50½; Ross, 16½; Shrewsbury, 75½; Stroud, 9; Taunton, 78; London, 104½.)

As the town nearest to the lowest bridge across the River Severn, Gloucester has had a chequered history. It was known to the

Romans, and its cathedral was once the church of a Benedictine abbey. The New Inn is a pilgrim's hostelry dating from the 15th century. The town makes a good starting-point for the Forest of Dean and for the picturesquely scarped and wooded part of the western Cotswolds.

SHREWSBURY TO HEREFORD

The Manchester or Liverpool cyclist who is heading for the lower Wye Valley, the Forest of Dean, or South Wales, has one of the finest and fastest main roads in the country to follow after Shrewsbury (see page 109 and also *Cycling Guide No. 2, Wales*). There is also a youth hostel at Shrewsbury.

The town should be left by way of English Bridge and Belle Vue Road. Soon the open country is entered and the road begins to climb steadily past Dorrington. The immediate surroundings are very picturesque, and next the finely-shaped hills of West Shropshire begin to rise round about. Without any steep climbs or falls, the road worms amongst them and enters **Church Stretton**, a small town finely situated in a valley amongst great hills. To the west climbs the delightful Cardingmill Valley, while, towards the east, the attractive Wenlock Edge district offers many short cycling excursions. Westward rises the grand district about Bishops Castle, described in Cycling Guide No. 2.

Beyond Church Stretton the route runs through charming valley scenery past Little Stretton and Marshbrook to Craven Arms, an important crossroads and a gateway to the romantic Forest of Clun district to the west.

One mile south of Craven Arms, to the west of the road, lies the picturesque fortified manor house called **Stokesay Castle**. The route goes up and down through quiet hill-and-dale country into Ludlow.

LUDLOW. M.D., Mon. E.C.D., Thurs. (Birmingham, 39½; Bridgnorth, 20; Church Stretton, 15½; Hereford, 24; Kidderminster, 22½; Leominster, 11½; Much Wenlock, 20; Shrewsbury, 29; Stratford-on-Avon, 53½; Worcester, 31½; London, 141 miles.) The town occupies one of the finest sites in the Kingdom, bordered on

PLATE I

The Winnats Pass, west of Castleton, Derbyshire.

PLATE II

**Gawsworth Church between Macclesfield
and Congleton, Cheshire.**

PLATE III

The fortified gateway on Monnow Bridge, Monmouth.

PLATE IV

The view from Symonds Yat, looking over the River Wye.

PLATE V

Welbeck Park, near Worksop, a typical scene in the Dukeries.

PLATE VI

A glimpse of Ledbury, Herefordshire.

three sides by the Rivers Teme and Corve. The castle was founded by the Normans, and the remains still dominate the town, together with the nearby church. The Feathers Inn, with its ornatelycarved timber, is one of the show places of the West Midlands. The outlet towards the south—followed by the route—leads down to the ancient bridge across the river. From this point there is a memorable picture of Ludlow. (There is a youth hostel here.)

The road southward leads through agricultural country by Wooferton into **Leominster.**

LEOMINSTER. M.D., Fri. E.C.D., Thurs. (Birmingham 47½; Bromyard, 11½; Gloucester, 26½; Hereford, 13; Kidderminster, 30; Ludlow, 11½; Monmouth, 30½; Shrewsbury, 40; Worcester, 26; London, 136½ miles) an old town with black-and-white houses. The Town Hall and Butter Market are amongst its other "sights."

Leaving Leominster by South Road, the journey is uneventful for 4 miles to Hope-under-Dinmore. Ahead lies the mile-long ascent of **Dinmore Hill**—the climb can be avoided by a slight detour, but is well worth while because of the view from the summit of the hill—from which there is an extensive prospect over the woodlands and fields. A fall of a mile on the south side and an undulating road lead into Hereford.

HEREFORD. M.D.,Wed. E.C.D., Thurs. (Abergavenny, 24; Aberystwyth, 79½; Birmingham, 53; Cardiff, 54½; Cheltenham, 37; Chepstow, 34; Gloucester, 31; Kidderminster, 35; Monmouth, 18; Oxford, 79; Ross, 14½; Shrewsbury, 55; Worcester, 26½; London, 132.) The pleasantest of the cathedral towns of the West Midlands and situated on the River Wye, to whose lower course it is the gateway from the north and Midlands.

WELLINGTON TO LUDLOW

The cyclist from Manchester or the Potteries who has reached the crossroads a few hundred yards east of Wellington (see page 82) has an interesting stretch ahead if he is making for Ludlow or Craven Arms on the way to Midland South Wales.

WELLINGTON. M.D., Mon., Thurs., Sat. E.C.D., Wed. (Birmingham, 32; Bridgnorth, 14½; Chester, 42; Lichfield, 30½;

Llangollen, 40½; Much Wenlock, 11½; Newcastle-under-Lyme, 29; Shifnal, 6½; Shrewsbury, 11½; Stafford, 21; Stone, 23½; Warrington, 55; Wem, 16½; Whitchurch, 22; Wolverhampton, 19; Worcester, 42; London, 141 miles.) The handiest place for the climb of The Wrekin, 1,335 ft., 2½ miles south-west. The hilltop is covered in woodland, but is actually a hard, sharp ridge, commanding wide views across the Severn Valley and into Wales.

From the Cock Inn crossroads the through way is southward, through industrialized Lawley and Coalmoor to the steep, winding descent of 1½ miles into **Coalbrookdale,** a cradle of industry, but in a situation which is naturally picturesque and not without its peculiar interest.

At the foot of the hill the way is rightward alongside the River Severn (just south is Ironbridge, where the iron bridge, erected in 1779, was the first of its kind in the world), through the deep Severn Gorge for a short way to the bridge across the river near Buildwas Abbey, on the west side. There are extensive ruins here.

The route next begins a steady rise of 3 miles through a lovely wooded valley, and then emerges into **Much Wenlock**, an old market town, with abbey ruins and a half-timbered Guildhall.

Continuing, the route goes along the side of wide Corvedale, with the tree-clad slopes of Wenlock Edge on the right and the shapely outlines of the Clee Hills on the left. To the north lies Wilderhope Youth Hostel.

The remaining part of the run towards the south-west leads through a series of charming villages and hamlets sheltered under the southern face of Wenlock Edge. Typical is Bourton, with an old hall, and as interesting is Shipton. At Diddlebury there is a church containing much Saxon work. After the hilltop fork at Pedlars Rest the road descends from the hills and the remainder of the route into Ludlow is along more level ground. Wellington to Ludlow by this route, is 31 miles.

HALESOWEN TO BRIDGNORTH
AND ATCHAM

The town of Halesowen, 7½ miles south-west of Birmingham, makes a starting-point for a hilly alternative route to the usual one between Birmingham and Shrewsbury via Wolverhampton and Wellington. London riders making for North Wales by way of the Shakespeare Country could link up with the route at Stourbridge or Bridgnorth after passing through Alcester and Bromsgrove. There is industry at first, but later the route brings in the Severn Valley and the Roman city of Uriconium.

From Halesowen the route is up and down and industrial as far as Stourbridge, but afterwards it becomes pleasant although hilly as it runs past Stewponey. Nearby Kinver Edge has fine views and rock dwellings. The village of Enville promises brighter country ahead, and the subsequent miles do not disappoint. Across the deep trough of the Severn Valley, which draws closer on the left, the rough moorland country to the west can be seen rising in great folds.

BRIDGNORTH. M.D., Sat. E.C.D., Thurs. (Birmingham, 26½; Chester, 56½; Church Stretton, 20; Craven Arms, 21½; Kidderminster, 13; Ludlow, 20; Shrewsbury, 21½; Stourbridge, 14; Wellington, 14½; Whitchurch, 36 | ; Wolverhampton, 14; Worcester, 27½; London, 134 miles.)

Buildwas Abbey.

A nobly built town—or rather two towns, one by the Severn and the other high above it—commanding an important river crossing. A resort for Black Country day-trippers, yet with plenty of interest.

A leaning tower forms the sole remains of a Norman castle. There is a half-timbered market hall, a Midland feature, built on stone arches. A steep hill leads from the bridge, through the lower town, and up past the castle into the upper town.

Leave by High Street and Northgate and follow the steep undulations of the road west of the River Severn into Ironbridge and over the bridge and past Buildwas Abbey and through the Severn Gorge by Leighton to Wroxeter, the nearest village to Uriconium and its Roman remains. Turn left at the Holyhead road and cross the River Severn over the new bridge at Atcham, whence it is 4 miles into Shrewsbury and rather less to the start of the southern by-pass round the town and to the youth hostel between this point and the centre of Shrewsbury, near Lord Hill's Column.

Birmingham to Shrewsbury by this route, 48 miles; by direct route through Wolverhampton and Wellington, 44 miles.

WEST OF THE SEVERN

There is some excellent quiet cycling country west of the River Severn between Bewdley and Bridgnorth. The former is an old town which is the gateway to the district from the south-west. The river can be approached at Arley and Hampton Loade, at both of which places there is a ferry.

The best headquarters for a thorough exploration of this area is perhaps **Cleobury Mortimer.**

CLEOBURY MORTIMER. (Birmingham 28; Bridgnorth, 14; Hereford, 34; Kidderminster, 11; Leominster, 21; Ludlow, 12; Shrewsbury, 35½; Worcester, 20½; London, 132 miles), a picturesque townlet with castle earthworks and the remains of a market cross. To the west rises Clee Hill, an area which offers plenty of scope for exploration.

A useful alternative route from Wellington and Bridgnorth southward runs along the west side of the River Severn instead of along the east as the main road through Worcester does.

From Wellington (see page 83) this alternative reaches the Severn at Coalbrookdale (see page 107) and continues into Bridgnorth. The Cleobury Mortimer road must be followed first and the southerly direction maintained to Billingsley. A series of deep lanes runs east from here to the primitive ferry at Hampton Loade—pedestrians and bicycles only. Beyond Kinlet, with its fine park, the route passes through Buttonbridge and enters the Forest of Wyre, a wide belt of woodland through which the road goes before gaining the old town of Bewdley.

The route passes through Ribbesford and becomes fairly level except for two sharp hills near Noutards Green, and soon reaches Henwick, a suburb of Worcester on the west side of the Severn. On the right side the Malvern Hills rise grandly. Past Powick, where left, the road reaches the side of the river at Rhydd and passes moated Hanley Castle. **Upton-on-Severn,** where there is a bridge across the Severn, has quite a foreign look, doubtless because of the appearance of its church, and thereafter the highway draws away from the river as it traverses lonelier farming country by Long Green, Hartpury and Maisemore before entering **Gloucester** (see page 98).

This route is a useful alternative link between Manchester and Gloucester, for Bristol and the West Country, and is only a few miles farther than the usual route through Worcester.

Cycling in the West-Central Midlands today

As Harold Briercliffe wrote this cycle route guide in 1949, many of the roads he mentions are now busier than they were and are not suitable for cycling today. Suggested alternative cycle routes, from Sustrans, which are in the same location as Harold's original route are listed below. To devise your own detailed route and map in the region, go to www.sustrans.org.uk.

There are two major National Cycle Routes in this part of the Midlands (National Route 5 and 45). **National Route 45** is fully opened and signposted between **Bridgnorth** and **Twyning Green** just south of Worcester. This route also runs via Stourport-on-Severn and Droitwich. The 60-mile route incorporates a converted railway path through the Wyre Forest and it follows the UK's longest river, the Severn. The route takes in much of the Worcester-Birmingham Canal and many miles of meandering minor roads through beautiful countryside.

The West Central Midlands is home to some wonderful parts of **National Route 5**, including the **Trent and Mersey Canal Route** that runs through **Stoke-on-Trent** down to Stone and on to Stafford. South of Stafford, National Route 5 picks up again in the **Chasetown Park**, which offers water skiing, sailing, angling and a steam railway. The route then continues into **Walsall** before reaching the heart of Birmingham.

Useful maps and books (available from www.sustransshop.co.uk): *AA Cycling in the Midlands; Cycling Traffic Free – Midlands and Peak District.*

CHAPTER VI

THE EAST-CENTRAL MIDLANDS

THE great area stretching southward from the River Trent to the River Ouse and westward from the Great North Road as far as Banbury contains a wealth of touring interest. The countryside is itself the most typically "English" in England—that is, it is a countryside of fields and woods and church spires. Except for a few corners like Charnwood Forest in the far north of the area, the district is all cultivated, and some parts of it are spoilt by mining. Coal is mined in Charnwood Forest, but far more destructive is the ironstone mining of much of the district. The huge open-cast shovels shear off the surface earth and leave long trails behind them which give the countryside the appearance of having been plagued by locusts.

Yet throughout the district there are belts of great charm, where old-world serenity still remains. Nevertheless, the district is not a touring area in the accepted sense. The cyclists of Nottinghamshire, Leicestershire, Northamptonshire, Bedfordshire and Huntingdonshire may use the countryside close to them for day and weekend runs, but neither they nor others would think of touring continuously in it.

The tourists who travel across this great inland area are generally bound for some other objective: for London, or the Cotswolds, or the East Coast, or Yorkshire, or the Lake District. Yet, because of the absence of river estuaries and mountains, the district is one of the pleasantest in England for across-country riding, being similar to Cheshire and North Shropshire in this respect. Amongst so many alternative routes, the plotting of passages across the district, avoiding main roads, becomes a major pleasure.

In the circumstances, however, the tourist is best directed to the most outstanding of the areas and to some of their features, and then advised to use a good half-inch map to find his way around.

The backbone of approach roads to the whole area is the London-Derby-Manchester road via Luton, Bedford, Kettering, Leicester and Derby. East of this, the Great North Road (see also pages 139–146) is useful. On the west side, the London-Coventry-Birmingham highway is too busy with heavy traffic to contemplate

113

as a route for the cyclist. Farther west the highways are quieter. Some of the routes through the Chilterns to the Midlands are given on pages 153–155.

CHARNWOOD FOREST

In the far north-west corner of the district lies Charnwood Forest. This is a miniature hill range, with granite outcrops and woodlands and wide views. It can be conveniently approached from Leicester through Groby, on the Ashby-de-la-Zouch road.

By turning right at Groby, **Groby Pool**, a haunt of many water birds, can be passed on the left, and then the pretty village of Newton Linford entered. There are facilities for meals hereabouts. To the north-east lies Bradgate Park, which has heathland and good viewpoints. By taking the left fork at the north end of Newton Linford, the grounds of ruined Ulverscroft Priory can be reached in 1½ miles. Next go north-east to Woodhouse Eaves and then travel westward from the inn at its north end by Copt Oak to **Bardon Hill**, the highest point in the Forest, 912 ft. above sea level. Just south lies the Ashby-de-la-Zouch-Leicester main road, along which the traveller can either return to Leicester or go on to the Potteries and the North or to Birmingham. The round of about 30 miles from Leicester to Leicester is full of interest.

SOUTHWELL

Rather to the north-east, west of Newark, lies Southwell, not far from The Dukeries. There is an excellent youth hostel here at Burgage Manor, a Georgian manor house, which has room for 80. The pride of Southwell is its Minster, which has Norman arches and much good wood carving. The cyclist travelling along the Great North Road—and tiring of it—could turn off at Long Bennington, north of Grantham, and follow lanes across country past Cotham Station, Elston and East Stoke—crossing the lonely Ermine Street—and then take the ferry at Fiskerton for Southwell—an unorthodox and quiet approach. Otherwise he can turn off at Newark. Southwell is about 132 miles from London.

RUTLANDSHIRE

The tourist travelling southward along the Great North Road who finds himself in Grantham (see also pages 145–146) has some pleasing country to hand if he cares to desert A1. There is, moreover, a youth hostel at Harrowby, on a hill just east of Grantham, and at 19 Welby Street, which runs parallel with the main street and just west there is a popular cyclists' house of call, Mrs. Melia's (the name should be noted carefully).

From Grantham the way is towards the south-west along A607 in the direction of Melton Mowbray. At first this rural highway skirts the hills, but after 5 miles it begins to climb to the roof of the wolds. As it leaves Lincolnshire and enters Leicestershire a wide prospect opens towards the Vale of Belvoir. Prominently situated and comparatively close at hand is the tower of **Belvoir Castle**, standing on the edge of a spur of hill.

At the crossroads at the village of Croxton Kerrial, the way is left across upland country past Saltby to Sproxton, a scattered village with an out-of-the-world look, and still southward by Edmondthorpe and Wymondham Station. (The alternative route through Coston is rougher, and the "waterfall" on the map is a geographer's joke—it is a mere tipple out of a dam.) Through Wymondham the road enters the Vale of Catmosse by the hamlet of Teigh and the tree-shrouded village of Ashwell. The road runs on the floor of the vale and around its edge rises a rim of hill upon which hang villages. Burley, to the west, has a great hall in a wooded park.

Oakham, which is next entered, is the quaintest and smallest of county capitals, vying in this respect with Appleby. There is a castle and mound, an old butter cross and an old school-house, now a museum; but the tourist will prize Oakham for its quietness.

Beyond the level crossing at the west end of the town a by-road strikes south-west through Braunton to an isolated crossroads neat Withcote. By going southward (to the left) here some of the loveliest parts of the East Midlands can be found. These are the woods and valleys of Launde Abbey (the building itself is private). A stiff hill leads southward from the secluded hollow of Launde and the road becomes a deep, winding one which emerges in the village of **Loddington**, a rambling, stone-built place in a well-watered valley.

There is an excellent youth hostel at Loddington, a large stone house at the west side of the village. The hostel is 30 miles from Grantham, and is an excellent centre for the unsophisticated area of East Leicestershire, with its breezy wolds and tangled valleys.

The Butter Cross
OAKHAM

ROCKINGHAM FOREST AND THE NORTHANTS UPLANDS

Loddington Youth Hostel can be used as a halting-place for those travelling southward over by-roads. Next day there is a chance of seeing a corner of Rockingham Forest, which once covered much more ground than it does to-day.

From Loddington the way is south-west along a narrow up-and-down lane which passes through a watersplash and then emerges on the Leicester-Uppingham road at a crossroads (**Uppingham,** 3 miles east, is a pleasant stone-built town on a hill). At this crossroads the way is straight ahead along a lane which keeps to the west side of the Eve Brook and wanders on into the hamlet of Stockerston. This is all remote country with cheerful streams and many woods and fields.

Still keeping south, along an uncoloured by-road, the route approaches Corby Reservoir, the only large sheet of water in a wide area, and therefore a magnet for wading birds. The last time I was there I saw a crane. In winter gulls are always present. The road keeps to the west side of the reservoir and then climbs to a by-road which leads leftward into the old-world village of Great Easton. "Short cuts" are in evidence here across to Rockingham village, but the wisest course is to go round by Rockingham Station before crossing the River Welland to the foot of **Rockingham's** steep main street.

The houses march steeply uphill from an old butter cross, and are of the russet-brown texture which makes so many of these Northamptonshire villages so charming (the stone is, however, that same ironstone which is so eagerly sought by the maws of the huge open-cast grabs). The houses have thatched roofs and pretty gardens, and they rise in a pleasant curve to the right of which stands the rebuilt church from which there is a wide view northward across the Welland Valley. At Rockingham, too, is the hospitable P.R.H.A. house, the Sondes Arms, handy for overnight stops or meals.

More notable, however, is Rockingham Castle. This crowns Rockingham Hill, and is the oldest house in Northamptonshire which has been consistently lived in. It was begun in William the Conqueror's time, and the keep was destroyed in the Civil War. The oldest work in the building dates back to the 13th century—the medieval bastion towers. Dickens spent some time at Rockingham, and was fascinated by the castle. There is a beautiful Elizabethan hall, with a minstrel gallery and an iron chest said to have belonged to King John.

Lady Culme-Seymour, the present owner of the castle, admits parties of cyclists to the grounds and the castle at a small charge. She has also helped cycling in another way by permitting massed-start races in the grounds on a small circuit—another appreciated gesture, for which clubs in the district are grateful.

Once up Rockingham Hill there comes a choice of routes. One useful route to London lies along the Kettering road for 3 miles to Great Oakley, there turning left by Newton to **Geddington**, where stands Queen Eleanor's Cross, the most carefully preserved of all the crosses erected during a funeral march of 150 miles between Harby, in Nottinghamshire, and London. The slender cross has old cottages, and the tower and spire of the parish church as a background. Over the River Ise passes an old stone bridge next to a ford. **Kettering** can be by-passed on the south-east. As this route crosses A6, the London-Manchester-Carlisle road, Wicksteed Park, a paradise for children and their parents, stands on the left, a pleasure haunt competently managed by the Wicksteed Trust. This route to London now undulates through the busy town of Wellingborough, old but now with many manufactures, and then runs southward to **Olney**, in the Ouse Valley, a perfect little townlet of stone with associations with Cowper. From Olney it is an easy run into **Newport Pagnell**, with its fine church and old-world atmosphere, and then by Woburn Sands to Woburn and A5 at Hockcliffe, on the Coventry-London road (see page 96).

From the head of Rockingham hill, however, there is a second choice. This leads leftward and into the startling town of **Corby,** a miracle of modern industry. Here a new town has arisen well within living memory. Its blastfurnaces are fed with the diggings of the huge shovels which are evident for many miles. A few of the old houses of Corby remain in the old part of the town.

By going left at the first T-road, and then right at the next, the edge of the mining trenches are passed and Stanion entered. Then the industry seems to fall behind and one arrives at **Brigstock,** as quaint and enchanting a village as there is outside the Yorkshire Dales. Its delightful old cottages and its tree-covered green with a quaint Elizabethan cross marks it out as a pleasant place for a halt. There is Saxon work in the church, for the village was something of a fortified outpost.

Below Brigstock the valley of Harpers Brook runs between low hills and passes neat villages at Sudborough and Lowick. The next village, **Islip**, is on the River Nene, and there is some yachting activity. The Manor House is a good call for meals and overnight stays.

Just across the Nene by an old causewayed bridge lies the small market town of **Thrapston** (on the edge of the ironstone area), which has touches of quaintness.

From Thrapston the route climbs high, and on the ridge before Bythom enters Huntingdonshire. The next important road turning leads rightward through Catworth and past Kimbolton Station into **Kimbolton**. The townlet is one of those sleepy places which have lost their former importance and gained in repose and beauty. The wide main street reaches up to the imposing gates of Kimbolton Castle. At the other end of the street stands a spired church in the Decorated style. The whole layout will remind the tourist of Eire. There is a connection: Kimbolton grew to importance and added to its buildings in the 17th and 18th centuries, when parts of Ireland were being developed on English lines.

At Tilbrook (1¼ miles west of Kimbolton) there is the hospitable Braemar Cafe, a cyclists' calling-place, and there is another, the "Beehive," at Ellington, 5 miles north-east.

The road eastward leaves Kimbolton through a narrow, kinked street, and runs through feathery woodland and farm country, past pretty Stonely and the wide, sloping main street of Great Staughton, to Crosshall, north-west of St. Neots, and on the Great North Road (see page 143).

The rider wishing to see more of Rockingham Forest should make the youth hostel at Kings Cliffe or the inns at Apethorpe, Bulwick, Deenethorpe or Rockingham his headquarters. Quite close to Kingscliffe—itself a rambling old townlet of many quaint corners—there are plenty of attractions. Outstanding is Stamford, on the Great North Road, perhaps the most fascinating small main-road town in England, a place built almost entirely of stone, and with many old churches and inns (see page 145). Nearer lies the site of **Fotheringay Castle,** associated with the tragic Mary Queen of Scots. **Blatherwycke** is a delightful village, with lakes and willows and old houses and halls on the Willow Brook. Bulwick, close by, is charming, too, while along the lanes north-west and south-east of the village are the few substantial remnants of Rockingham Forest. The course of the Welland between Rockingham and Stamford is studded with attractive stone villages: Collyweston, Ketton, Easton-on-the-Hill and Duddington amongst them. South east of Kingscliffe lies **Oundle,** a town famous for its school, but also for fine houses, a noble church, old inns and an air of dignity.

On the west side of Kettering there is a youth hostel at Broughton, which could be used as a base for the exploration of the Nene Valley district. To be noted thereabout are **Rothwell**, on the Kettering-Leicester road, where there are thousands of human bones and skulls in the crypt; other attractions are main-road towns like Higham Ferrers; the splendid Saxon tower of **Earls Barton**; and another Eleanor Cross at Hardingstone, south of the county town of Northampton. West of Kettering the serious tourist might penetrate to the high ground near Naseby, north-east of which stands the monument commemorating the battle in the Civil War. In Naseby, too, is a spring over a garden wall reputed to be the source of the River Avon. There is also a ruined tithe barn in the village.

Cycling in the East-Central Midlands today

As Harold Briercliffe wrote this cycle route guide in 1949, many of the roads he mentions are now busier than they were and are not suitable for cycling today. Suggested alternative cycle routes, from Sustrans, which are in the same location as Harold's original route are listed below. To devise your own detailed route and map in the region, go to www.sustrans.org.uk.

National Cycle Route 6 is the arterial route that runs north to south through the Central and East Midlands. Just over 100 miles of this route separate Milton Keynes and Derby, passing through Northampton and Leicester. This stretch features some real cycling gems, including the 16-mile converted railway path between Northampton and Market Harborough. Further north, the route guides riders to a whole network of recently built traffic-free cycle paths around Watermead Country Park. The Park is a popular hot spot for fishing, walking, cycling and watersports. The 140-hectare park is a haven of wildlife, water and lush pastures and is now connected with cycle and walking routes to help people reach the park without driving.

Other great Sustrans routes in the East-Central Midlands are **National Route 64** and **National Route 1**, heading east to west through **Lincoln**. The **Dukeries Trail** converted railway path enters Lincoln from the west. Heading east, the **Waterlink Railway Line** is lined with wonderful sculptures.

Useful maps and books (available from www.sustransshop.co.uk): *South Yorkshire & the Peak District cycle map; AA Cycling in the Midlands;* and *Cycling Traffic Free – Midlands and Peak District.*

Currys are at your service EVERYWHERE!

Every ★
is a Currys
branch

It's comforting to know, when you're touring, that you are never far from a Currys' branch. Each is *THE* CENTRE FOR *CYCLES* in the locality and is the one place where you can be sure of getting *any* accessory you want. In case of need, always HURRY TO CURRYS!

Currys
LTD
THE CENTRE FOR CYCLES

CHAPTER VII

THE MALVERNS, WYE VALLEY AND FOREST OF DEAN

THE city of Worcester makes a good starting-point for a tour of
the hill, gorge and woodland scenery which stretches south-
westward as far as Newport, Monmouthshire. It is not a wholly wild
district like Mid-Wales, nor bare and grey like the higher parts of
the Cotswolds.

Instead the character of the area has been marked since early
prehistoric times by the presence of two great rivers, the Severn and
the Wye. It is a border district, a debatable land, and as such is
reminiscent in its scenery and associations of the Scottish Borders.
Indeed, the Malverns are more than the Eildons of their district,
while instead of one noble river, the Tweed, there are two. Besides,
the district is perhaps the most heavily wooded hill-and-dale country
in the west of England. Abbeys and castles, fortified houses and
quaint towns also give to the region a variety that is not easily found
elsewhere at so close a distance to London. Of heavy industry there
is practically nothing, if the occasional mining smirches to be found
in the Forest of Dean are excepted.

APPROACHES

For all places north and east, and even from London, Worcester is
the best starting-point for a tour of the district. It is readily accessible
by road and railway from London and Birmingham, and therefore
from Manchester, Liverpool, the East Midlands and the West
Riding.

From London a picturesque road approach, introducing Edgehill
and the Shakespeare Country and avoiding the direct speedway
through Aylesbury and Bicester, is to travel through Hemel
Hempstead, Leighton Buzzard, Linslade, Winslow, Buckingham,
Banbury and over Edgehill (see Cycling Guide No. 6) to Kineton

and Stratford-on-Avon (see page 96), where there is a youth hostel.

From Stratford it is a pleasant rural ride through Alcester to Worcester, or, better still, by the more secluded byway route past Binton Station, Wixford, Dunnington and Flyford Flavell.

Routes from Manchester and Liverpool to Worcester will be found on pages 84–85 and 96–99. The best approach from Leicester and Nottingham lies through Hinckley, Nuneaton (a useful starting-point for an exploration of the "George Eliot" country, south-west of the town, around Arbury Park), Fillongley, Meriden, Solihull and Redditch, or, alternatively, through Rugby, Warwick and Stratford-on-Avon.

Road routes towards the south-west are always a problem from the West Riding towns. The brave will take their industries and hills first and make for Worcester through Holmfirth, Glossop, Hayfield, New Mills, Disley and Whaley Bridge. After the latter place it is a hilly but pleasant run by Rainow to Macclesfield, from which town the way south-westward lies through Congleton and Talke, as described on pages 84–85.

There are several useful youth hostels in the area covered in the tour, notably the new one opened in 1948 at St. Briavals, on the east side of the Wye, and in the Forest of Dean. This is the best youth hostel centre for the Lower Wye. The district has a long tradition of countryside catering, and is now offering services which are comparable in most respects (except prices) with conditions before the war.

Riders who find themselves in Worcester at the start or the end of a tour should remember that a little way to the west lies some of the pleasantest country in the West Midlands, in the Teme Valley.

To reach the best part of this valley the Bromyard road should be followed for 9 miles to Knightsford Bridge. Instead of going left across this, the by-road climbing to the right should be followed over Ankerdine Hill and Berrow Hill to the village of Martley. By going left here the well of the valley can be followed under picturesque wooded slopes and with a fine succession of views across the river at the bold-fronted range of hills to the north-east. At Ham Bridge the rightward turn must be taken and the west side of the valley followed past Shelsley Walsh village, where the famous motoring test-hill climbs leftward as a cul-de-sac with a gradient of 1 in 5.

At Stanford Bridge the traveller is only a little east of the pleasantly-situated village of **Stanford-on-Teme.** The through route turns rightward, however, and crosses the bridge before traversing Kingswood Common and reaching Great Witley, a village in a picturesque spot below the green and brown billows of the Abberley Hills.

Witley Court, with a beautiful park, lies to the south. The return journey to Worcester can be varied by taking the road past Little Witley to Holt Heath—close to the bridge across the Severn at Holt Fleet, for Ombersley, Droitwich and Birmingham or Stratford-on-Avon—and then by Grimley and Hallow.

This round from Worcester is about 30 miles, and takes the greater part of a summer's afternoon and evening.

From Stanford-on-Teme a valley road keeps to the south of the Teme and makes for Tenbury and the crossroads at Woofferton, on the Ludlow-Leominster road.

A SIX-DAY TOUR
(From and to Worcester—167 miles)

Leave Worcester (see page 123) by St. Johns and Malvern Road, and follow the road through Powick to Bastonford and Newland. Here the climb into Malvern begins, and leads by Malvern Link to the side of the Malvern Hills. Instead of going left, however, into **Great Malvern** the road climbing gradually round the northern face of the hills should be followed into Malvern West.

The Malvern Hills rise splendidly from the Severn Valley and form a long, impressive ridge which completely dominates the scenery of this part of Worcestershire. The ridge is, in fact, a mountain range in miniature, rocky and green and windswept, with magnificent views in every direction. The prospect westward from the road described is altogether delightful, a patchwork of field and forest and hill stretching away in a thousand folds and undulations to Hereford and beyond.

From West Malvern a by-road runs high on the west flank of the hills and skirts the highest point of the range, the Worcestershire Beacon, 1,395 ft. It is worthwhile to hide the bicycle and make the climb to the summit on foot. The view is wide and inspiring in all directions.

From the road, as it keeps to its perch, the westward panorama continues. About two miles from West Malvern the route crosses that which descends from the Wyche Cutting. This is the main Great Malvern-Ledbury road (an alternative main-road route to the one being described), and after crossing it the route becomes more rural as it goes through Broad Green and joins another main highway, A48. On following this south-west for a short way, an entrance to Eastnor Park will be seen on the left. The private road through the park can be used by cyclists (not motorists). It is rough in parts, but follows a delightful course along The Ridgeway. At first there is pretty woodland on either hand, but later open parkland is gained before re-entering woods. On the left there is a charming little valley throughout. The road emerges at the old-world village of Eastnor, in a delightful hollow on the Tewkesbury-Ledbury road. The way is rightward into Ledbury.

The townlet of **Ledbury** (20 miles from Worcester by this route) is a delightful tourists' haunt, with several places where meals may be obtained. It has a market hall on stilts and several old inns and half-timbered houses and a pleasant environment. The imaginative will find in this area that touch of mediaevalism which always comes amongst settlements in well-watered, well-timbered and long-tilled countrysides. It is a fairy-tale land, distantly reminiscent of Hans Anderson. Or perhaps it is only the half-timbered houses!

From Ledbury the tourist should next continue towards the south-west, following the undulations of A48 past Ludstock to Much Marcle. A right turn here leads through lanes to **Rushall**, where there is a youth hostel in pleasant, off-the-beaten-track surroundings (Malvern to Rushall, 26 miles). Bed-and-breakfast tourists should keep along the main road to Ross-on-Wye, 7½ miles beyond Much Marcle, with half the journey uphill and the other half downhill, the easiest section last.

From Rushall the hosteller should climb to the village of Marcle

Hill, then making for Barrel Hill and the Hereford-Ross road at Cross-in-Hand. At a height of about 500 ft. there is a grand view across the River Wye at one of its wide sweeps. From this point the route runs southward and then south-westward by Old Gore and along A48 into **Ross-on-Wye** (35) A description of the town appears on page 136.

Ross is the northern gateway to the most picturesque and best-known part of the Lower Wye Valley. There is no continuous road down the valley between Ross and Monmouth, although the roads on the east and west sides approach the river closely. The beauty spot of this section of the Wye is **Symonds Yat**, a deservedly popular point where the river forms a great loop divided by a neck of high ground, and is only about 300 yds. across. Coldwell Rocks, just east of the Yat, form perhaps the most impressive piece of scenery on this reach. The only way to see the river fully between Ross and Monmouth is by boat. Even the journey by railway between the two places shows far more than the few peeps obtainable from the roads. The route given is necessarily a compromise—perhaps the best course in all the circumstances, as the trip by boat from Symonds Yat to Monmouth is fairly expensive, although it is possible to take bicycles on the journey.

From Ross, which is left by Copse Cross Street, the journey of 3½ miles to Kerne Bridge is obviously in the valley, although out of sight of the river until the last few hundred yards to the bridge, in which the Wye reveals itself as a wide, noble flood, backed to the south-west by a wooded ridge.

Across Kerne Bridge, about a mile to the west, are the fine ruins of Goodrich Castle—well worth visiting. At Kerne Bridge there commences, down the east bank, a lovely riverside run of 3 miles to Lower Lydbrook. Thereafter the road southward climbs steadily up a ridge high above the river into **English Bicknor,** on the northern edge of the Forest of Dean. Beyond the village a lane goes rightward and emerges on a more important road running northward to **Symonds Yat**. This road should be followed rightward for rather more than a mile. On the way the deep Wye Valley squeezes the ridge closely on both sides, owing to a great, narrow loop.

The best prospect lies to the right, or east, and from this perch,

500 ft. above the river, there is a magnificent double view. To the west there is a grand picture of the gorge and of the opposite bank rising to the hill called Great Durward. Northwards there is a more open view along the Huntsham peninsula. Down below, on the east, is the river flowing at the foot of the Coldwell Rocks and, farther to the east rise the ridges of the Forest of Dean.

The cyclist who wishes to return to Ross can descend from the viewpoint to the riverside at Symonds Yat Station, and then retrace for some way before taking the road by Huntsham Bridge and Pencraig back to Ross (Symonds Yat to Ross, direct, by this route, 7½ miles).

The viewpoint is everything at Symonds Yat, and the through tourist need not descend to the riverside and reverse his route up the toilsome climb back to it.

From the viewpoint the outward route should be retraced along the ridge running southward and then Christchurch entered. Here the tourist is entering the area of the Forest of Dean. Unlike some other mining areas, the district is not greatly spoilt by pit workings, because few mines have normal pit-head gear. The activities of the miners hereabouts are on a relatively small scale, although the earth has been worked for coal for centuries. The predominating tree is oak, and, after the New Forest, the Forest of Dean is one of the largest stretches of woodland in southern and western England.

In 1938 the Royal Forest of Dean was formed into the first of Britain's National Forest Parks. Wherever possible the Commission's woodlands are open to the public. In all, 15,000 acres are controlled by the Commission, and there are additionally wide stretches of commons and heaths.

At **Christchurch** is a camping ground established by the Forestry Commissioners. It is 700 ft. above sea level, and there is a splendid view from its timber pavilion. The camping ground covers 14 acres, and is one of the best "regulated" sites in the country. It is one of the finest centres for exploring the lower Wye and the Forest of Dean, and campers who stay there for a few days can readily adapt the excursions given for hostellers and bed-and-breakfast tourists to their requirements.

The pavilion has large-scale maps of the district, and the facilities for boiling water (costing 1d.) and for making meals (4d.) are very useful in rainy weather. The atmosphere of the pavilion resembles that of the "self-cooking" Scottish hostels.

Tent fees vary from 1s to 1s. 6d. per night, according to the size of tent. There are reduced prices for longer stays. Facilities available include water supply, washing huts and lavatories. There is no need to book in advance, and further information may be had from the Deputy Surveyor, Forestry Commission, Whitemead Park, Parkend, Lydney, Gloucestershire. The Christchurch camp site is some 20 miles from Gloucester along the Gloucester-Monmouth road, and is, therefore, about 124 miles from London, 65 miles from Birmingham and 46 from Cardiff.

Beyond Lower Berryhill the road southward reaches the small town of **Coleford**, a handy place for hostellers and others buying their own provisions. Still going southward along B4228, the route passes through high farming country, with few woodland patches, and then reaches **St. Briavels** (55).

A little north-west of the village stands the large and impressive youth hostel of **St. Briavels Castle**, opened in 1948, with accommodation for 60 (summer months only). The castle stands in a prominent position, and the two round towers which flank the main doorway date from about 1130 A.D. There are remains of a moat, while the commanding view towards the west looks across the Wye Valley at the Sugar Loaf and the Skyridd Mountains above Abergavenny. The castle was at one time the administrative centre of the Forest of Dean. Inside there are wide 13th-century fireplaces and a wheel which turned a spit and was revolved by a dog.

The hosteller is recommended to stay at St. Briavals for two or three nights. The bed-and-breakfast tourist should be able to find accommodation in the Wye Valley, about Llandogo, some three miles west of St. Briavels.

The first, most obvious, excursion from St. Briavels is an exploration of the lower Wye Valley between Monmouth and Chepstow. Between these two towns, for a distance of 16 miles, river and road keep within close distance of each other, so that the tourist can see from the saddle the splendours of the most accessible part of the lower valley.

From St. Briavels the tourist should first go back along the Coleford road for about two miles to Trow Green, there turning leftward past Clearwell, with its 14th-century village cross and a park, into the pretty village of Newland. Thereafter the road begins to descend steadily towards the Wye Valley. About 1½ miles farther on, however, a by-lane climbing rightward into Staunton should be carefully sought. Staunton (not to be confused with the Herefordshire Staunton) is a village amongst woodlands on the main . Gloucester-Monmouth road. On meeting the latter, the way is leftward towards Monmouth.

A short way west of the village, and in a wood on the left (or south) rises the hill on which stands the Buck Stone. This is a notable viewpoint marked by an old red sandstone conglomerate rocking stone called the **Buck Stone**. The hill is 915 ft. above sea level, and from it the prospect, even in a district of noteworthy viewpoints, is a remarkable one, second only to the better-known one from the Wynd Cliff, lower down the valley. From the Buck Stone the view extends westward far into Wales and northward to the Clee Hills in Shropshire. The deep valley below, the chequered fields and the wooded heights, all backed by the summits and ridges of Wales, combine to compose an unforgettable picture.

Just west of the Buck Stone is another hill called Kymin, from which there is a better view of the Wye Valley foreground around Monmouth. This hill is, however, less accessible from the road than the Buck Stone. It forms a pleasant evening walk from Monmouth, however, lasting about 1½ hrs. return. Kymin is 700 ft. above sea level, and is crowned by a naval temple commemorating old-time sea heroes.

From near The Buck Stone there is a splendid winding drop of nearly three miles into **Monmouth** (66), entered by the Wye Bridge and St. Mary's Street. The town is situated where the River Monnow joins the Wye, and lies in a pleasant district. Further details are given on page 136.

Monmouth should be left by the Wye Bridge again, and the east bank followed through pretty—but no more— scenery past

Redbrook and on to **Bigsweir Bridge**, where the Wye becomes tidal. Here the hosteller is only 2½ miles from St. Briavels again, the hostel being at the top of a steep climb. The bridge is crossed and then the valley begins to wind and becomes more interesting. The road is excellent. At **Llandogo** the river presses the road below a steep hill, and thereafter there is a slight rise to Coed Ithel before descending past Bigsweir and, after Tintern Station, winding round a great loop which leads to **Tintern Abbey** (77).

The abbey stands between the road and the Wye, and is perhaps the most beautiful monastic ruin in England. Its natural surroundings, too, challenge comparison with those of Bolton Abbey, Yorkshire. The abbey was founded in 1131, and was rebuilt in the 13th century in the Decorated style. The west doorway and a grand west window are amongst its most impressive features. The ruins and the grounds are very well kept.

Beyond Tintern Abbey the road begins to rise towards the climax of the Wye scenery—the reason why the journey is taken down the river instead of up, as is normally best. This natural climax is the Wynd Cliff, and if this were visited first, all else on the lower Wye would appear inferior.

The road ascent from Tintern Abbey continues steadily for 2 miles to Moss Cottage. Throughout there are peeps through the trees at the Wye as it churns through its bed. Even from Moss Cottage, which lies at the base of the Wynd Cliff, the picture formed of the river in its great coiling valley is memorable.

Bicycles should be left at Moss Cottage and the ascent made of the **Wynd Cliff,** which is the culmination of a long line of tree-clad limestone crags rising above the road. A small charge is made for admission. A climb of some 300 steps leads from the "cottage" to the summit, which is 800 ft. above the river and 917 ft. above sea level.

The Wynd Cliff viewpoint is a platform fenced by a parapet at the summit of the perpendicular cliff which overlooks the River Wye. The prospect is a grand and far-reaching view, extending over nearly all south Monmouthshire and eastward across the Wye and the Severn into Gloucestershire and Somerset. Immediately below is the Wye in its deep gorge, with, farther east and separated only by a narrow neck of land, the wide estuary of the Severn. The bowl formed by the richly wooded cliffs of the Wye is the outstanding feature of the view. In late autumn the picture is like a Rubens palette. Scots tourists will be reminded of the view from Kinnoul Hill, Perth.

On regaining, the bicycles, the road should be followed as it climbs by the walls of Piercefield Park into **St. Arvans**, a hilltop village. A descent of 2 miles alongside the park leads into **Chepstow** (82), described on page 136.

Tourists who have traversed the Wye Valley between Monmouth and Chepstow have a useful alternative route by Trelleck, to the west, if they wish to get away from the busy road along the valley. It does not match the valley route in interest, but is quiet and rural.

Passing under the West Gate and down the main street of Chepstow, the tourist should make for the bridge across the Wye. A little south-east the river is crossed by the railway tubular bridge, built by Brunel in 1862. This has a total length of 600 ft., of which the main span is 300 ft. There are exceptionally high spring tides here, 38 ft. being the average rise, but 70 ft. has been recorded.

Beyond the road bridge the highway twists and climbs, passing, on the right, the road leading down to Beachley for the ferry to Aust (see page 135). About two miles out of Chepstow a left turn leads down the Lancaut isthmus, which should be visited. Beyond Wye Cottage there is a turn to the right, beyond which it is a short walk to the **Lancaut Double View,** on the Ban-y-Gor cliffs, from which there is a splendid low-level picture of the Wynd Cliff to the north-west, and also of the Twelve Apostles Rocks under Piercefield Park, to the west. The ruin on the east bank is that of Lancaut Church.

On regaining the Coleford road the climb continues up Dennel Hill, from which there are again fine views across the river. (A walk of 1½ miles to the west leads to the Devil's Pulpit, from which there are more beautiful glimpses of the valley.)

When once the woods of Tidenham Chase are gained it is easier going past Hewelsfield into St. Briavels again (92).

This route makes a very full day of 37 miles. Suitable halting-places for meals are: "Elevenses," Monmouth; lunch, Tintern vicinity; tea, Chepstow.

The next day should be devoted to the district to the north-east of St. Briavels, the Forest of Dean, which with its steep undulations, little valleys and dense foliage contrasts with the previous trip through the Wye Valley. The interests of the Forest are less sophisticated than those of the valley, and there is more serene enjoyment for the cyclist who loves the quieter ways.

From St. Briavels the lane running eastward from the village and into **Bream** (95) should be followed at first.

The next section leads northward and into the Forest, passing Whitemead Park, local headquarters of the Forestry Commission. On reaching B4431, on the edge of the Park, the way is rightward along this road, soon following it leftward and through the deep woodlands—one of the prettiest parts of the forest—past the Barracks to **Blackpool Bridge** (100). Here stop to examine a section of exposed Roman paving, used by the invaders for hauling coal. The Lancashire traveller will be reminded of the Roman road across Blackstone Edge, between Rochdale and Halifax. Next return to the Barracks and just beyond turn rightward past Fancy Colliery to a beautiful stretch of road leading to the Speech House, or meeting-place of the forest courts, where disputes are settled by the holders of rights in the area. A steep drop leads west over a railway to a crossroads. Here it is worth while going leftward for about a mile down the valley as far as the foot of Cannop Pond for the sake of the views. Returning to the crossroads, the way lies northward, keeping close to the stream for some way before emerging on the Gloucester-Monmouth road. At this the way is leftward, still in the woodlands, past Mile End to Coleford and St. Briavels again (116). This run of 24 miles through the Forest of Dean is only one of the many woodland outings which can be devised from St. Briavels.

Returning from St. Briavels towards the north, the tourist will probably wish to see more of the Forest. This can be done by following the previous route to Bream and there making for Breams Eaves, Pillowell, and over more by-lane routes to Viney, Nibley and **Blakeney** (126), the latter being on a main road into South Wales from Gloucester. From this point the side-road running northward up a valley past Ayleford should be used. The surroundings of the road are picturesque but have plenty of mineworkings, especially as **Cinderford** (132), the "capital" of the Forest, is reached. At the next crossroads, at Nailbridge, the way is rightward into **Mitcheldean** (136), formerly an important market town, and now an old-fashioned place. There is a youth hostel in the centre of the town.

Just north of St. Michael's Church, in Mitcheldean, a byroad strikes rightward off B4224, and leads along the edge of a commanding ridge past Lea Line to Aston Ingham, and then into the old townlet of **Newent** (143), with its 16th-century market house. From Newent an up-and-down road goes northward to **Dymock** and **Ledbury** (151) again.

From Ledbury the course of A48 should be taken along the east side of the Malvern Hills to Malvern Wells and to the Malvern Youth Hostel at Peachfield Road, between Malvern Wells and Great Malvern Road. Malvern (158).

From Malvern it is a straightforward run back to **Worcester** (167).

Londoners who have reached Mitcheldean and wish to travel directly home through Gloucester can do this readily by following A4136 and A40 into Gloucester (Mitcheldean-Gloucester, 11½ miles), and then making for Cheltenham, Witney and Oxford.

THE SEVERN BORE

The natural phenomenon of the Severn Bore may be seen and heard best between Newnham, on the west, and Elmore, on the east bank of the river, at the high spring tides.

This tidal wave may be seen as low down the estuary as Guscar Rocks, at Woolaston, and it increases in size as the river bed narrows past Sharpness. Opposite Awre, on the west side, the estuary contracts to about a quarter of its width a little lower, and as the tide meets the current it pushes it upstream as a tumultuous wall of water. This wall travels upstream at 12 miles per hour, and reaches a height of some three feet in the centre and as much as five feet at the banks. The noise is a rumble in the distance, but becomes a tumult nearby.

Perhaps the best place to see the Severn Bore is at the Stonebench Inn, east of Elmore, some 4½ miles south-west of Gloucester.

CROSSING THE RIVER SEVERN

Sooner or later nearly every tourist who visits the Wye Valley is confronted with the problem of crossing the estuary of the River Severn. This difficulty is likely to continue to arise until the river has a road bridge well below Gloucester, where is at present the lowest bridge on the river.

There is a vehicular ferry taking bicycles between Beachley, about four miles south-east of Chepstow, and Aust, 5 miles from the Bristol-Gloucester road at Almondsbury. The service, while quite adequate and reasonable in price, is at the mercy of the tides, and on occasion there are inevitably considerable delays.

On the whole the crossing which is most useful to the cyclist is by the Severn Tunnel. On the west side the station is at Severn Tunnel Junction, about 7½ miles south-west of Chepstow. On the east the first station is at Pilning, which is handy enough for a rider going northward, or making for the east through Wotton-under-Edge and Tetbury. For those travelling southward, for Devon and Cornwall, for instance, the best plan is to book right through to Bristol (Temple Meads), thus avoiding traversing the busy northern suburbs of Bristol and much of the central part of the city.

The rider who has finished his tour of the Wye Valley at Chepstow and wishes to reach London quickly will find that his most practicable course is to ride to Newport and from there take one of the through expresses to Paddington.

The Severn Tunnel was opened for passenger traffic in December, 1886, and took 13½ years to build. Including approaches, it is 7½ miles long, but the actual tunnel is less than 4½ miles. The total cost was about two million pounds.

Higher up the Severn, the ferry between Newnham and Arlingham is too close to Gloucester to have any advantage to the cyclist. The Severn Railway Bridge, between Lydney and Berkeley is more useful, the stations being Severn Bridge, on the west, and Sharpness, on the east. There are about eight trains daily on weekdays in both directions, the first being about 7.15 a.m. from Severn Bridge and 8.30 from Sharpness, and the last about 8 p.m. from Severn Bridge and 8.45 from Sharpness.

GAZETTEER

CHEPSTOW. M.D., alternate Tues. E.C.D., Wed. (Abergavenny, 25; Cardiff, 28; Gloucester, 28½; Hereford, 34; Monmouth, 16; Newport, 16; Pontypool, 21½; London, 132½ miles.)

The town is at the mouth of the River Wye, where it enters the Severn. The castle is an outstanding feature. The remains include a Norman keep, round towers and three inner courts. The West Gate of the town is part of the town wall. There is a youth hostel in Chepstow, at St. Lawrence, half a mile west of the town on the Mounton Road, and also other accommodation in the town.

The cyclist staying at Chepstow and wishing for a run in quieter country than the Wye Valley should consider exploring the tract of country which lies to the west of the town, around Went Wood and Earlswood Common and as far as the Usk Valley. This is all rural Monmouthshire, relatively unknown as a touring ground.

MONMOUTH. M.D., Fri. E.C.D., Thurs. (Abergavenny, 17; Brecon, 37; Builth Wells, 50; Cardiff, 36; Chepstow, 16; Gloucester, 25; Hereford, 18; Ludlow, 42; Newport, 24; Ross, 11; Tewkesbury, 36; Usk, 13½; Worcester, 40 (direct); London, 129.)

Monmouth is situated where the River Monnow enters the Wye. The bridge over the former stream has a Norman gatehouse and is very impressive. There are the ruins of a castle also. The town has several places catering for cyclists.

ROSS-ON-WYE. M.D., Thurs. E.C.D., Wed. (Abergavenny, 23; Cardiff, 47; Chepstow, 25; Gloucester, 16½; Hay, 30; Hereford, 14½; Monmouth, 11; London, 121 miles.)

Perhaps the most attractive of the towns on the lower Wye. It has a West-Midland feature in its market hall dating from the 17th century. There are also several old houses. From the Prospect, adjoining the churchyard, there is a fine view of the River Wye as it coils around a horseshoe bend. Ross makes a useful centre for the Wye Valley.

Cycling in the Malverns, Wye Valley and Forest of Dean today

As Harold Briercliffe wrote this cycle route guide in 1949, many of the roads he mentions are now busier than they were and are not suitable for cycling today. Suggested alternative cycle routes, from Sustrans, which are in the same location as Harold's original route are listed below. To devise your own detailed route and map in the region, go to www.sustrans.org.uk.

The longest section of fully open National Cycle Network Route in this area is **National Route 42**, running from **Chepstow** up to **Hay-on-Wye** via **Abergavenny**. This is a challenging but spectacular route that runs over the **Gospel Pass** (at 540 metre/1,476 ft) before descending into Hay-on-Wye from the south. Another currently unconnected part of National Route 42 runs on forestry tracks through the Forest of Dean. The Forest offers a huge range of cycling from extreme down hilling to gentle family saunters. There is also a well-equipped cycle centre with cycle hire and a café.

A wonderful route in this area is the **Peregrine Trail** that runs just over 8 miles from **Monmouth** to **Goodrich** via **Symonds Yat,** crossing the Welsh-English border. This route includes a few miles of traffic-free path, which offer stunning views of the River Wye and a possible sighting of a Peregrine Falcon.

Useful maps and books (available from www.sustransshop.co.uk). *Celtic Trail East cycle map.*

IN GOOD COMPANY

Royal
Enfield
BICYCLES
THE ENFIELD CYCLE CO. LTD., REDDITCH

CHAPTER VIII

NORTHWARDS FROM LONDON

FROM the cyclists' point of view, the most important highway leading northward out of London remains the Great North Road. The earliest importance of A1 arose because it was the shortest way to Edinburgh and because of the ancient attraction of York as an ecclesiastical and trading centre. The rise of large-scale industry in the 19th and 20th centuries sent the bias over towards the west, to Manchester, Liverpool and Birmingham, and to A5 along the line of Watling Street, a route which was already familiar as the road to Ireland.

Even the rapid growth of the towns of the West Riding has not been sufficient, in the past 30 years, to lift the importance of A1 as a great commercial highway to the level of A5. There is plenty of through and local traffic along A1, but it remains, especially now that the Barnet by-pass relieves it so much, the quietest of all the main roads going north from London. At New Hatfield the old and the new roads are together for a while, but at the foot of Digswell Hill there is another parting, and the country highway through Codicote to Hitchin and on by Henlow to Girtford Bridge or Bedford is relatively light in traffic density.

In this survey of cyclists' routes going north from London, I will use the course of A1 as a basic route, switching over to the Ware-Royston road, and then moving back to A6 by St. Albans to Bedford, and to A5 by Dunstable and Towcester, together with the variations on these routes. All the country east of Royston will be dealt with in a forthcoming book on the Eastern Counties; all west of Aylesbury comes into the "Thames Valley and Cotswolds" section of the next book in this series, "Southern England."

THE GREAT NORTH ROAD

I propose to deal at some length with the Great North Road because of its historical associations and because many of the younger generation of cyclists as they ride north are quite unmindful of the part played by the road in history—in cycling history, too. The details here are necessarily sketchy and are meant as an introduction only.

Fifty years ago the open country began at Whetstone; now the traveller must pass through Barnet before reaching it. In the centre of **Barnet** A5 goes off, rather unceremoniously, to the left, while A1 tends to the right. Soon the latter is crossing Hadley Green, and then reaches Hadley High Stone, commemorating the Battle of Barnet, fought on Easter Day, in 1471, in which the Lancastrians were beaten by Edward IV. The stone was erected in 1740. Soon afterwards, just before Gannie ("Ganwick") Corner, comes the highest part of the road south of York, and only 13 miles from London.

The modern suburb of **Potters Bar** is named after a toll-bar which formerly stood at the north end of the village. From this point into Hatfield the road has changed very little in 50 years, and an old-timer finding himself on it and neglecting the improved surface and the few new houses and the masts of the Brookmans Park wireless station, would soon get his bearings.

An older Great North Road runs to the left and regains the modern highway at Bell Bar. Hereabouts there are cyclists' calling-places at the "Marshmoor" and the "Merrythought" cafes. The remaining miles into Hatfield are sandwiched between the fine park of the Cecils on the right and the main East Coast railway route to the north. The general inclination of the road from Ganwick Corner is downhill, and the entry into the narrow main streets of **Hatfield** is a fast one. Hatfield has few things to delay the cyclist these days— once it was quite a rendezvous—but it is worthwhile glancing up High Street, on the right. This climbs fairly steeply, and has an old-world air—it is missed by most passers-by—and once formed part of the main road. The great mansion of the Cecils is of red brick in Tudor Renaissance style, with a central clock tower. Hatfield is 20 miles from the General Post Office, London.

At the north end of the small town the road crosses the railway. Away to the left stretches the building development of New Hatfield, mostly concerned with the De Havilland aircraft factory. A little farther ahead the old road joins the new at the north end of the Barnet by-pass.

The next mile or so is uneventful, but at Stanborough, a

crossroads hamlet, a road goes rightward into Welwyn Garden City, a community which followed the pioneer Letchworth as a planned unit. To the left goes the old North Road into Lemsford, a picturesque village. The main road next rises steadily for 1½ miles into Ayot Green, and very quickly begins the descent of tree-aisled **Digswell Hill**, a drop of nearly a mile. This is the most picturesque bit of the North Road so far.

At the foot of Digswell Hill the old road bends left at a transport cafe, but the new sweeps rightward along a bypass through a pretty hollow, later marred by villas as is most of the remaining up-and-down road into Woolmer Green and Knebworth, the latter a modern growth around the railway station, a mile east of the old village of Knebworth, which is close to Knebworth House.

The main road next descends to Broadwater, and then continues as a wide and dreary highway towards Stevenage. On the way, however, on the right, are the "Six Hills", a series of prehistoric mounds.

Stevenage (London, 31½) has a wide main street. The old church lies on a hill to the right, close to the site of a former village which was destroyed by fire. In the rafters of the old Castle Inn lies the coffin and remains of Henry Trigg, whose will, proved in 1724, contained the provision that his body should not be buried but disposed of in that manner.

After Stevenage the country becomes lonely. Graveley is just a wayside village, and after it comes a sharp rise up Jacks Hill, said to have been the home of a giant called Jack, who lies buried at Weston, to the east. Nowadays the summit of the hill is surmounted by a petrol station and transport café.

The tall trees and chimneys to the left form part of the first garden city of **Letchworth**, founded in 1902, and for the most part well planned, with residential quarters to the west and an industrial section in the east, together with modern social amenities like libraries, swimming pools, cinemas, parks, commons and shops.

A bold range of chalk hills rises on the right before entering Baldock. These hills are crowned by beeches—outliers of the Chilterns. **Baldock** has a modern hosiery factory and a wide main street, together with an awkward corner at its foot. Here the way is rightward and then left at the traffic lights (straight on for Royston).

The next section of the road is undulating and not without interest, for woods fringe the road and there are charming farms and houses. Ahead, however, it mounts **Toplers Hill**, which has a water tower to the left. On the right are abandoned (temporarily) road-widening plans. Beyond the "Plough" Inn, on the hilltop, the road begins to drop. Here the Great North Road is only 225 ft. above sea level, but compared with what lies immediately ahead it is a considerable eminence. Particularly in winter, when the mist lies low on the levels, the tourist might be forgiven for thinking that he was gazing over a wide inlet of the sea. To the left runs the firm greensand ridge near **Old Warden**. To the right the country undulates. But straight ahead it is dead level—the famous Biggleswade market-gardening district. To right-central juts a bold greensand peninsula, seen from this distance even as a black cape because of the evergreens. There is every evidence that at no great distance in time these levels were all covered by the sea. Even now they are only 80 or 90 ft. above sea level—and 60 miles from the sea.

The drop past the Biggleswade waterworks and into Biggleswade is a fast one. **Biggleswade** (London, 45½) is a town amongst market gardens. At its north end a blacksmith, Dan Albone, established in the past century a flourishing cycle-making business. Close to the site of this is The Sun, a catering house which appeals especially to cyclists.

Beyond the bridge across the River Ivel, the Great North Road settles down for a stretch of mild going. Only the variety and nature of the growing produce betrays the richness of the surrounding land.

Approaching Girtford Bridge, a lane comes in from the left, and in the apex thus formed stands the **Bidlake Memorial**. This takes the form of a memorial garden and stones suitably inscribed. The memorial commemorates the late F. T. Bidlake, cyclist, timekeeper, writer, who died on September 17, 1933, following an accident on Barnet Hill, where he was knocked down by a motorist.

Girtford Bridge (London, 48¾) is a hump-backed structure built of russet stone, which carries A1 across the River Ivel. No place in England is as familiar to road time-trialling cyclists as this. In the long late-summer days long-distance cyclists compete with time and with each other, and this bridge is the focal point of their activities.

For many years before Hitler's War the house on the right, just across the bridge, called "Fuller's", was administered as a cyclists' calling-place by the Fuller's and their successors, the Ewing's. The building and its surroundings were always full of wheelmen at weekends, and the business must have been a profitable one.

The only comment that seems possible now is that the cycling world itself was slow in not taking over, in some form or another, the house and its old traditions and methods.

On the next stage A1 skirts the small town of Sandy, and then, after crossing a railway bridge, runs across a bleak stretch of farming land for nearly two miles into the roadside village of Tempsford, close to the meeting-place of the River Ouse and the River Ivel. The village is pleasantly shaded, and "The Anchor" at its north end forms a picturesque corner.

A bridge leads across the Ouse to the west bank, and then follows more open but easy going past the "Black Cat" roadhouse, and then come Wyboston and **Eaton Socon** (55¼), the "Eton Slocumb" of Dickens. A road goes rightward into St. Neots (see page 151), but the main highway bears leftward on a gradual climb, passing, on the left, an armless windmill, and then the crossroads at Crosshall, where a pretty road strikes off westward to Kimbolton (see page 119). A gentle drop into more wooded country and into Huntingdonshire leaves, on the left, an unobtrusive mineral-water works at a spring once renowned for its healing properties. The countryside begins to assume a pleasanter look. On the right lies Paxton Park, close to the meadows of the winding and widening Ouse. Southoe, to the left of the road, is a compact hamlet. Before entering **Buckden** (61¼) the road becomes more undulating, and is then confined between the crowding houses of this main-road village, with the ruined red-brick walls and towers of an old palace of the Bishops of Lincoln. The fortunes of the great George Inn declined when coaching traffic passed to the railways, but have revived in the cycling and motoring age.

A fork right at the north end of Buckden leads into Huntingdon (3½ miles—see page 148), but A1 dips leftward, and soon reaches the Sun Inn at Brampton Hut (the leftward road goes into Thrapston, 13½ miles). A length of well-watered country leads by Matcham's Bridge, so named because of the murder of a drummer boy in 1780 by a man named Matcham—the story was used in the Ingoldsby Legend, *The Dead Drummer.*

Through the two Alconbury villages, and then the highway starts to climb up **Alconbury Hill**, the first appreciable rise since Toplers Hill, south of Biggleswade, and about half a mile long. At the top of the hill (only 164 ft. above sea level) the Old North Road comes in from the right after passing through Ware, Royston and Huntingdon (see pages 110-113). There, too, is an ornate railed-in milestone.

The next stretch of road is a moderate descent down Sawtry Hill. Standgate Hole, on this, was formerly a great place for highwaymen. Nowadays all the stretch between Alconbury Hill and Norman Cross is scheduled for widening, but the work has been held up temporarily, as will be seen from the wide roadside verges.

There is little interest along this piece of A1, although there are wide views across the flats to the right. At Conington, down a lane to the right, there is a well-wooded park and a Perpendicular church. At **Stilton** (75½) a wayside village with a broad main street stands The Bell, an old stone inn. Here were brought from Wymondham, in Leicestershire (see page 115), the cheeses which became known as "Stilton".

At **Norman Cross** (76), where the main road into Peterborough forks rightward, is a large inn. The main road goes leftward, still with the Ermine Street, which came in at Alconbury, and past a useful transport café, into the pleasant village of Water Newton, close to the pools of the slow River Nene.

There is a new by-pass to the east of Wansford, but the thorough tourist will continue into the village of **Wansford** (84), crossing the River Nene by a narrow and ancient bridge, with 10 arches, and entering Northants.

Beyond Wansford the road becomes open once again. To the north-east lies Barnack, with a fine Saxon tower. At Barnack was quarried the building stone used in Ely Cathedral and other mediaeval churches and abbeys. A sharp drop and rise precede a splendid run alongside the ducal walls of Burghley Park.

Stamford (90), situated on both sides of the River Welland, is probably the best-preserved of all English main-road towns. It has few manufactures and no new suburbs, and wears an aristocratic air. There are six churches dating from the Middle Ages, and many old inns, notably The George. There is, too, the gateway of Brazenose College, set up here after a temporary migration from Oxford in the 14th century. There are also many striking stone houses. The stone came mostly from Barnack and from Ketton, both within a few miles of Stamford, which is in Lincolnshire.

In these days of fast and heavy long-distance traffic Stamford ought to be by-passed. Presumably this will come about some day, probably on the west side of the town. Nowadays the through traveller must pass along London Road, St. Martins, cross the Welland, go up St. Mary's Hill and twist round into St. Mary's Street, and up into Scotgate and the Casterton Road—quite a feat of manoeuvre for the driver of a heavy lorry.

Leaving Stamford, the returning Northerner will find a reminder of home in the stone walls. He is still on Ermine Street, and as he passes through Great Casterton he enters Rutlandshire. The next village, Tickencote, has a Norman church. A belt of trees ahead marks the site of the Battle of Empingham, in 1470. There is a glimpse of Exton Park on the left and then A1, which has been going northwest from Stamford, turns to the north and undulates along a quiet stretch of road. **Colsterworth** (103) is now by-passed by a new road to the east. Signs of ironstone mining become visible. There is another stretch of parkland on the left, beyond the golf course of Stoke Rochford, and then the prominent tower of Great Ponton is passed on the right.

Little Ponton is seen in a hollow on the right, and soon the road begins to descend steeply into Grantham, the former L.N.E.R. main line coming in also from the right down a steep fall.

GRANTHAM. M.D., Sat. E.C.D., Thurs. (Baldock, 74½; Bedford, 67; Birmingham, 70; Boston, 30; Cambridge, 64; Derby, 39½; Doncaster, 52; Kettering, 41; Kings Lynn, 54½; Leicester, 30½; Lincoln, 24½; Melton Mowbray, 15½; Newark, 14½; Northampton, 55; Nottingham, 24; Oakham, 20½; Peterborough, 34; Sheffield, 51½; Skegness, 52½; Sleaford, 14; Spalding, 31;

Stamford, 21; London, 111 miles.) An important road and rail centre and the largest town on the Great North Road between London and Doncaster.

The country lying east of the Old North Road and north of Grantham as far as Selby is described in "Eastern England", a forthcoming book in this series.

THE OLD NORTH ROAD

The old milestoned road between London and Ware runs through a succession of industrial and residential areas, by Kingsland Road, Dalston, Stoke Newington, Stamford Hill, Tottenham, Edmonton, Waltham Cross and Cheshunt, beyond these joining up with the New Cambridge Road. This old road, marked as A10, is always busy and congested, although relieved to some extent by the New Cambridge Road, a modern highway a little to the west. There is little of interest along the old road, which is comparatively level throughout, except the Eleanor Cross at Waltham Cross (where the Four Swans Inn has a sign across the road) and **Waltham Abbey**, a little east of the Cross. The abbey is the oldest Norman building in England, and is the burial place of King Harold, slain at the Battle of Hastings in 1066.

From north and north-west London, and even from Marble Arch (by Finchley Road and Golders Green), the best way to reach the New Cambridge Road is to strike the North Circular Road and to follow this until it comes to the New Cambridge Road (A108), north of Wood Green. The new road runs northward and meets A10 at Wormley, after which there is still plenty of traffic by Hoddesdon—close to Rye House, where the Rye House Plot was hatched in 1683 for the assassination of Charles II and his brother James. Nearby is the Rye House Inn, where is the Great Bed of Ware, which is 12 ft. square and made of oak. The road continues through Great Amwell, alongside the New River, and up the Lee Valley into **Ware** (22 miles from the Mansion House by the old road). The town is a picturesque place, with red-roofed malthouses, many trees and waterways, and an old church.

The main road traverses the town and then turns right-ward and northward to run over high ground before dropping to the hamlet of Wades Mill in a picturesque site on the River Rib.

A slight detour from the main route forms a pleasant (if involved and delaying) alternative here. It leads rightward by Thundridge and round to Great Barwick, where there is a very pretty ford amid woodland surroundings—one of the pleasantest and quietest spots near London. The through route can be regained by going northward from Great Barwick through the Rib Valley to Puckeridge.

On the rise from Wades Mill a stone obelisk commemorates Thomas Clarkson, who dedicated his life to the abolition of the slave trade. Farther on, a stone in a field marks the alighting place in 1784, of the first balloon to ascend in Britain.

Puckeridge (28) is a large village with a commodious youth hostel in the main street. A10 here bends leftward and soon, across the railway on the left, the rider enters the delightful old village of West Mill.

Buntingford (32½) has a long main street and is a small with one or two calling-places for meals. Beyond it A10 rises to higher ground commanding extensive views. Buckland is a farming village situated on the open wolds where the Ermine Street runs northward straight as a ruler. There is a drop into **Royston** (39), a country town and on the edge of Cambridgeshire. There are roadhouses and inns here. In the main street there is a curious cave in the chalk. This goes down to about 28 ft. below street level, and has some unusual carvings. Some 12½ miles north-east of Royston lies Cambridge.

The Ermine Street takes another of its curious bends, this time towards the west, at Royston, and along its line the road, now A14, is lonely. About four miles ahead the great double avenue of elms, nearly three miles long, leading up to Wimpole Hall can be seen on the right. Near Wimpole Lodge there is a café on the left catering for cyclists, and down the Cambridge road on the right there is another.

The road next climbs to higher ground, maintaining its directness and crossing the railway. **Caxton** village wears an old-world look, and beyond it is the crossroads at Caxton Gibbet. At Papworth there is a home for consumptive ex-servicemen, and soon the highway reaches the old town of **Godmanchester** (59), which has a pleasant air. The town has several old houses, but is really a southern annex of **Huntingdon** (60), to which it is joined by an old causeway and a bridge across the River Ouse. The road continues along a narrow main street.

Huntingdon was the birthplace of Oliver Cromwell. Across a picturesque little square to the left stands All Saints Church, where the details of the Protector's birth are preserved in the register of a church now demolished. On the right is the restored Grammar School, where both Cromwell and Pepys were educated. On the left, beyond the church, is the George Hotel, which has an unusual gallery, well seen through a wide entrance. West of Huntingdon, Hinchingbrooke House lies in a great park.

Beyond Huntingdon, the Old North Road along the Ermine Street runs by Great Stukely and Little Stukeley (where there is an inn traditionally associated with Dick Turpin), and up to the summit of **Alconbury Hill** (66), where the Great North Road is met (see page 144).

FAST BY-ROADS NORTH FROM LONDON

The least hilly of all the routes leading north and northwest from London is one running mostly over secondary roads from Hoddesdon by Hertford to Stevenage and Hitchin, for Bedford or for Girtford Bridge (see page 142).

Hoddesdon, on A10, just north of the point where the New Cambridge Road joins the old road, is the starting-point. Here a road strikes leftward and climbs past Hailey-bury College (well-seen on the right) and across Hertford Heath into **Hertford** (4½ miles from Hoddesdon), an old-fashioned town with some quaint nooks and corners. The route leads west along Fore Street, and then by dignified St. Andrew Street, soon passing Hertford North Station.

Over a short hill the road passes into well-watered parkland and, with the little River Beane on the right, reaches Waterford, a pleasing halting-place for cyclists. It has several catering houses. Through Stapleford the road drops to the side of the extensive and well-wooded grounds of Woodhall Park, on the right. The next village, Watton-at-Stone, is quite old-world, and at its south end an alternative route from Hoddesdon by Ware comes in.

The road continues as a well-surfaced by-road running through woodlands and past fields, and without steep rises or falls, until it reaches the Great North Road at Broadwater. The main road is then followed into Stevenage (see also page 141—15 miles from Hoddesdon).

At the north end of the long main street of Stevenage, opposite the Cromwell Hotel, the Hitchin road leaves A1 and goes through Little Wymondley into Hitchen (20).

Most of the town lies to the right of the road, but it is worth turning down Sun Street, past the lightweight bicycle depot of Sudbury Cycles, Ltd., owned by a well-known Letchworth and Hitchin cycling enthusiast, and into the town square. There are some picturesque alleyways near the large and interesting church, which has a broach spire, familiar in North Hertfordshire. To the east lie Letchworth (page 141) and Baldock (page 142).

Hitchin town square should be left by Brand Street and past the cattle market, after which a right turn leads in the direction of Bedford and Girtford Bridge.

The road leads northward, past the large R.A.F. camp around Henlow Station, and then, in Bedfordshire, makes for the townlet of Shefford, where the way leads rightward and up a gradual climb past a stretch of heathy woodland on the left before dropping smartly down Hammer Hill and continuing through Cotton End and by Cardington Aerodrome to the spreading southern suburbs of **Bedford** (37), a busy county town. Elstow, 1½ miles south, was the birthplace of John Bunyan.

BY-ROAD ALTERNATIVE TO A1

At Welwyn (see page 141) begins a by-road route which can be used as an alternative to the Great North Road as far as Alconbury Hill. This road is invariably preferred to the main road by Stevenage and Baldock by experienced cyclists going northward. To Girtford Bridge it is actually shorter than the main road.

At the foot of Digswell Hill, instead of going rightward with the main road, the sideroad bending left into the small town of **Welwyn** should be used. This leads down a short but steep drop.

Beyond Welwyn the highway climbs alongside a stream into Codicote (1½ miles from Welwyn) and continues to climb as far as the 28th milestone from London. On the right is an imposing gateway to Knebworth House. Lanes on the left lead pleasantly to **Whitwell**, a large village in which there is a good youth hostel.

There is some up-and-down going as the highway crosses the watershed, out of the London basin into the drainage area of the Ouse. The road is a rural one and has plenty of woodlands. Over to the west the hills rise in folds, some of them being well covered by trees.

The hamlet of Langley leads into Rush Green, and soon, on the right, a steep lane rises into the pretty village of St. Ippollitts. The entry into **Hitchin** is quite picturesque. There is no need to go to the town square, which lies to the right, and the road soon traverses a narrow street before emerging on a wider highway past a large open space on the right.

The next stretch of road is the most famous in the annals of early road racing. Countless road events and attempts on road records started just north of Hitchin. Nowadays the centre of gravity has moved to Girtford Bridge, but there are still alive many men who recall the great days of this stretch of road.

At Henlow Camp the former Midland Railway between Bedford and Hitchin is crossed (the main road goes left to Shefford and Bedford—see page 149). This line was formerly much more important, for until the railway between Bedford and London was completed all traffic from the Midlands came this way and used the Great Northern route between Hitchin and London.

Henlow village is still in the levels, and the usual route lies across the crossroads and along the Biggleswade road past Henlow church, soon turning leftward down a lane which runs just north of Clifton church and on to Stanford. An alternative to this route goes left at Henlow crossroads into Clifton village, there going rightward past Clifton church to the former route, which is joined at the crossroads north of the Church.

The Biggleswade road continues northward, over a stretch by a gravel pit formerly known as the Fair Mile, across the new bridge over the River Ivel and into Langford and Biggleswade.

The fastest through route to the north goes by the few houses of Stanford and then through a lonelier countryside, over all crossroads, and so to **Girtford Bridge** (see page 142).

To the left of the road between Stanford and Biggleswade lies a long greensand ridge which is well-wooded and full of picturesque charm, notably at the old-world village of Old Warden, where there is a great park.

The road from Girtford Bridge to Tempsford has been described on pages 142–143. North of Tempsford and just short of the Ouse bridge a road sidles rightward and keeps to the east side of the Ouse, past a large new electricity generating station and into Eynesbury, which is to St. Neots what Godmanchester is to Huntingdon, but is hardly as old-fashioned.

ST. NEOTS. M.D., Thurs. E.C.D., Tues. (Baldock, 19½; Bedford, 12; Cambridge, 17½; Ely, 31; Huntingdon, 9; Kettering, 28; Peterborough, 26½; London, 56 miles) has a very large market place and a church with a beautiful tower. At the west end of the square a 16th-century bridge over the Ouse leads across to Eaton Socon (page 143) and the Great North Road. There are several temperance hotels and inns at St. Neots and also a very lively cycling club.

The by-road northward from St. Neots leaves the square by the traffic light at the north-east corner, and then, after climbing a short ascent, reaches a viewpoint at **Paxton Hill** where the River Ouse and the railway are to be seen in the valley to the left, with fields and gentle hills in the background—a graceful scene and typically South Midland. Great Paxton and Offord D'Arcy are pleasing wayside villages, and afterwards the road runs over more open land and into Godmanchester for Huntingdon and Alconbury Hill (see page 148).

BY-ROADS TO ASHWELL

Another useful alternative to both A1 and A10 starts at the north-west end of **Watton-at-Stone** (see page 149), and runs through the shallow valley of the River Beane and into **Walkern**, a straggling village. Beyond the smaller village of **Cromer** the route reaches Cumberlow Green and continues northward past Rushden and Redhill before descending steadily to the Baldock-Royston highway at Slip End. Ahead now are the great fields to the south of **Ashwell**. The large village of Ashwell is one of the most interesting in Hertfordshire. Formerly it was of greater importance, as its handsome, broach-spired church shows. Close by there is an old half-timbered building now used as a museum. The spring which gives the village its name can be found at the east end to the left of the road. Here clear waters well up out of the earth and form a large pool. Trees form a surround to the pool, and the spot is a cool and pleasant one on a summer's day. Close to the spring is the "Three Tuns", which caters for cyclists. (Another cyclists' house is "The Six Bells", at Sandon, 3 miles east of Redhill on the approach to Slip End.)

From the west end of Ashwell a by-road forks towards the north-west and through Hinxworth reaches **Toplers Hill,** on the Great North Road (see page 142).

A QUIET ROAD INTO EAST LINCOLNSHIRE AND THE NORFOLK COAST

From the Plough Inn at the summit of Topler's Hill a lane strikes rightward and forms the beginning of a route which leads to Boston and King's Lynn, and is described fully in The Eastern Counties. The section of the route inside the scope of this guide passes to the east of the Great North Road over quiet side roads through Millow and near Dunton. At the crossroads east of Sutton village it is worth turning left to the ford and ancient pack-horse bridge at the far end of the place, returning to the through route afterwards.

At a T-road ahead the way leading left should be used, and at the church a sharp right turn taken past Gamlingay village and through Waresley and Eltisley villages to Kisby's Hut, on the Royston-Huntingdon road, which forms the easterly limit of this guide.

Afterwards the road leads through St. Ives, with its ancient bridge, and across the Fens to Crowland, for Boston, or by Ely to King's Lynn.

MISSING LUTON

The ancient town of St. Albans, 20 miles from London, is not only a converging place of several important roads from the south-east, south and south-west, but also a useful starting-point for a little-known stretch of the eastern Chilterns which lies to the north. The town stands on A6, but anyone travelling northward along this road must pass through the congested streets and extensive suburbs of Luton in order to reach Bedford. The best way to reach Bedford from London is through Hitchin, as described on pages 113-114. This alternative is not only less hilly but it is also quieter and more rural.

The great attraction at St. Albans is the cathedral, which stands on the west side of the town. The Cathedral was once the church of a great abbey, and it has most architectural styles, including Norman.

West of the Cathedral is the Abbey Gatehouse, dating from the year 1380, and from it a path leads to the River Ver, beyond which lies the site of the Roman city of Verulamium. This was founded soon after the Roman conquest, and fragments of the remains of the walls, a theatre and a town hall are visible. Close by is the Fighting Cocks Inn, one of the oldest in England.

From St. Albans the busiest road for motor transport in England, along A5, runs through the narrow streets of Redbourn and Markyate Street to **Dunstable,** the nearest town to Whipsnade Zoo, to the south-west.

Beyond Dunstable the main road runs through the chalk by a deep cutting, and then goes on in long undulations by Hockliffe, Fenny Stratford, Stony Stratford, Towcester, Daventry and the Coventry by-pass, for Birmingham, Manchester, Liverpool and the North.

A5 is much too busy for the touring cyclist. However, a useful alternative is given on pages 154–155.

From St. Albans the tourist wishing to miss Luton and to see a secluded corner of the Chilterns, should turn off A6 at the north-east side of the town and run by Sandridge and across commons into the old-fashioned small town of **Wheathampstead**. A steep drop leads to a stiff rise under the railway and beyond this the climb continues into rural country at Gustard Wood and soon into old-world **Kimpton**. This district has so far escaped suburbanization, and its winding lanes, old cottages, and alternating stretches of breezy upland and pleasant valley are all stimulating.

Still going northward from Kimpton, the lane route climbs to high ground again, passing a water tower, and then descending, into delightful **Whitwell**. (There is a youth hostel at the east end of the village.) The way northwestward out of Whitwell should be followed, first up a shallow valley in which watercress is cultivated. Then a secluded lane heads for Lilley, leaving unlovely Breachwood Green to the west and pretty Kings Walden to the right. On meeting the Hitchin-Luton main road the way is left, briefly, to Lilley, where right and northward again.

The piece of open country beyond Lilley village is delightful, all patches of woodland and wide pasture. Soon the lane reaches a summit, with the hill of Pegsdon Beacon on the right. Next comes a fall down a long lane. On the left, hidden by plantations, stands Ravensburgh Castle, while ahead the undulating lowland begins to unfold. At the foot of the hill is a crossroads, the rightward road leading through the avenue called the "Golden Mile," and over pleasant country into Hitchin, with the route leftward leading, first, through other woods, and then under a bold chalk escarpment into **Barton-in-the-Clay**. This village is on the Luton-Bedford road (A6), 6½ miles north of Luton and 13½ miles south of Bedford. The road to the county town runs pleasantly enough past Silsoe Park and into the scattered townlet of Clophill, on the greensand, and therefore with plenty of evergreens in its vicinity. The remainder of the way into Bedford lies through similar scenes, in which meadow and woodland alternate.

ALTERNATIVE TO A5

The most useful alternative route to A5 from the west side of London for tourists wanting a quiet way to the Midlands and the North lies by way of the Watford by-pass. The simplest outlet from Marble Arch lies along the Edgware Road until, some 12 miles out, the crossroads just beyond Brockley Hill is gained. Here the way is leftward, past Aldenham Reservoir and along the broad new road to Hintonbridge, south of King's Langley, some 20 miles from London.

Over two miles farther on, at Apsley End, a road goes rightward through Hemel Hempstead and continues up the pleasant valley of the River Gade, reaching, on the left, the youth hostel at Piccotts End, some 25 miles north-west of London, and a handy halting-place for the night.

A little farther on, at Water End, is one of the most picturesque riverside vistas in the Chilterns. The road continues to be interesting through the valley, past Little Gaddesden, and crosses the chalk uplands before descending smoothly by the Travellers Rest (there is another hostel at Tring, to the west), and through Billington into the town of Leighton Buzzard (London, 38 miles). Features of the town are the graceful spire of its church and its market cross.

From Leighton Buzzard a road, A418, runs northward, crossing A5, into the Georgian townlet of **Woburn**, on the greensand in a district of green hills and dense evergreens. Woburn Park, to the east, has access by means of a public road. In the park there are herds of deer and other animals. Beyond the east side of the park a network of interesting lanes can be traversed by Harlington and Sharpenhoe to Barton-in-the-Clay (see opposite) for Luton, St. Albans and London.

From Leighton Buzzard there is a pleasant series of secondary roads through Stewkley, which has a church with much Norman work, by Swanbourne to the country town of Winslow, and then into **Buckingham**, formerly the county town of its shire, and nowadays quiet and out of the world.

Leaving the town by the Brackley road, the going is still rural. To the right is Stowe Park and Stowe House, the latter now a school, but with a frontage of 900 ft.

Brackley betrays the nearness of the Cotswolds, with its tree-lined, sloping main street, which is traversed on the route by going leftward, downhill and then rightward.

The Banbury road has several interesting villages, notably Farthinghoe and Middleton Cheney. Banbury is described fully in the next volume in this series, but the through tourist sees it as a bustling country town.

From Banbury the tourist making for the north should go along A41, past the stone-built village of Warmington and by Chesterton Hill, with its curious windmill, into Warwick, for Birmingham and for the North, by Stonebridge.

TOWCESTER TO WARWICK

Another useful by-lane link leads across from Towcester, on A5, to Warwick. This starts immediately north of the stream and railway at Towcester, and then runs through a series of picturesque villages linked by unfrequented lanes through Greens Norton, Blakesley, Maidford, Preston Capes (particularly charming), Charwelton Station, Priors Marston, and so to Southam for Leamington, Warwick and Birmingham, or for Stonebridge and the North. This route forms another country alternative to a part of A5.

Cycling North of London today

As Harold Briercliffe wrote this cycle route guide in 1949, many of the roads he mentions are now busier than they were and are not suitable for cycling today. Suggested alternative cycle routes, from Sustrans, which are in the same location as Harold's original route are listed below. To devise your own detailed route and map in the region, go to www.sustrans.org.uk.

The National Cycle Network has its own version of the Great North Road, which exceeds the A1's reach: **National Route 1** runs for over 1400 miles from Dover up to the Shetland Islands via London, Newcastle, Edinburgh, Inverness and many other towns and cities along the route. National Route 1 is known better by the shorter, named sections of which it comprises. **The Coast & Castles Cycle Route**, for example, runs from Newcastle up to Aberdeen via Edinburgh and takes in some truly wonderful scenery, including the spectacular Northumberland coast.

National Route 1 running through North London is better known as the **Lea Valley Cycle Route**. It provides a largely traffic-free 20-mile connection from the Docklands up to Cheshunt. This route runs past the 2012 Olympic Park and is just one of many routes being developed by Sustrans and many other organisations in the capital as a part of **London Greenways**.

The **Norfolk Coast Cycleway (Regional Route 30)** is one of Southern England's most popular cycle routes, which runs roughly 97 miles from Great Yarmouth to Kings Lynn. This Area of Outstanding Natural Beauty is relatively flat and is lined with many quiet country lanes, bridleways and tracks, making it an ideal spot for cycling.

Useful maps and books (available from www.sustransshop.co.uk): *AA Cycling in London; The Norfolk Coast Cycleway; Yorkshire Wolds, York & Hull cycle map; Three Rivers cycle map; Coast & Castles South cycle map; Coast & Castles North cycle map;* and *Aberdeen to Shetlands cycle map.*

APPENDIX

Sustrans Cycle Mapping

> • View 25,000 miles of cycle routes, including 13,000 miles of National Cycle Network online using Sustrans interactive mapping. Visit: www.sustrans.org.uk/map

You can also:
- Draw your routes, measure distances and share your favourite journey with others.
- Find local amenities including bike shops / hire centres, shops, schools and local attractions.

See every bus stop and train station in the UK with links to their timetables.

The Complete National Cycle Network App

Access our online mapping from your pocket with the Complete National Cycle Network app. The app includes all of our online features as well as:
- GPS tracking – record your route and share it with friends
- Store the map backgrounds for an area when you have no mobile signal

INDEX